W9-CPW-922

# Summer Smarts for Cool Kids

### Over 150
### Fantastic and Fun
### Learning Activities
### to Help Kids Beat the Summer Blahs

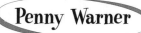

Penny Warner

Prima Publishing

For Tom, Matthew, and Rebecca

Copyright © 2002 by Prima Publishing, a division of Random House, Inc.

All rights reserved. No part of this book may be reproduced or transmitted in any form or by any means, electronic or mechanical, including photocopying, recording, or by any information storage or retrieval system, without written permission from Random House, Inc., except for the inclusion of brief quotations in a review.

Published by Prima Publishing, Roseville, California. Member of the Crown Publishing Group, a division of Random House, Inc.

PRIMA PUBLISHING and colophon are trademarks of Random House, Inc., registered with the United States Patent and Trademark Office.

All products and organizations mentioned in this book are the trademarks of their respective companies.

Interior illustrations by Paula Gray.

**Library of Congress Cataloging-in-Publication Data**
Warner, Penny
  Summer smarts for cool kids : over 150 fantastic and fun learning activities to help kids beat the summer blahs / Penny Warner.
      p.    cm.
  Includes index.
  ISBN 0-7615-3747-3
  1. Educational Games. 2. Activity programs in education.  I. Title.
LB1029.G3 W34 2000
371.33'7—dc21                                              2002022180

02  03  04  05  DD  10  9  8  7  6  5  4  3  2  1
Printed in the United States of America

First Edition

Visit us online at www.primapublishing.com

# Contents

# Acknowledgments

Many thanks to the following parents and students who contributed their wonderful ideas for summer fun: Kaveh Amini, Deb Barges, Priscilla Hopkins, Maureen Gin, Melody Johnson, Nancy Kindley, Christy Kuhner, Teresa Lau, Colleen Miller, Ann Parker, Barbara Swec, Susan Warner, and Allie Young.

And a special thanks to my editor, Jamie Miller.

# Introduction

"I'm bored!"

"There's nothing to do!"

"Can I watch TV?"

After months of school, extracurricular activities, homework, and regular routines, summer vacation has finally arrived. You've all been looking forward to a more relaxed schedule, lots of free time, and especially to a long break from homework. Surely your creative children will find plenty to keep themselves active and entertained throughout the summer.

But instead of "Let's play a game!" you hear "I'm bored!" How can they be bored already?

Instead of "I've got an idea!" you hear "There's nothing to do!" There are *lots* of things to do!

Instead of "I'm going outside!" you hear "Can I watch TV?" Is that all they can think of?

*Summer Smarts for Cool Kids* is here to save your summer by keeping your kids cool, captivated, and stimulated while school's out. The following twenty chapters are filled with exciting and fun activities, games, sports, and play ideas to lure the kids off the couch—and away from the TV and videogames.

You'll find over 150 ways to help kids improve their reading skills, enhance their vocabulary and language development, learn about scientific properties, practice their math skills, use their brains for problem solving, enjoy nature study, build up their bodies, improve their fine and gross motor development, use their creativity and imagination, and even make money doing chores and small jobs.

*Summer Smarts for Cool Kids* includes chapters on sharing quality time with the family to enhance family values and chapters filled with games and activities to share with friends to increase kids' social skills. You'll even find a chapter that offers kids ideas for what to do when you're at work and they're home alone, to help build their confidence, competence, and independence. The book also offers ideas for what to do while traveling on the family vacation, having fun at the beach, and camping in either the wilderness or the backyard. You'll find plenty of outdoor activities to keep the kids outside and exercise their bodies. And when it's hot outside, you'll appreciate the suggestions and recipes for keeping cool, including frosty snacks, water fun, and pool play. And to keep the kids engaged during those long summer nights, we provide a whole chapter of nighttime activities.

Each activity has a suggested age range. These ranges are only suggestions. You know your child best, so please read each activity to make sure it's appropriate for your child's level of development. Some of the activities can be simplified to accommodate younger children, while others can be made more challenging for older children. Some activities are fun no matter what age your child is and can be adapted to fit his or her abilities and interest. In general, activities for three- to six-year-olds require adult supervision, activities for seven- to nine-year-olds need adult approval, and activities for ten- to twelve-year-olds should have adult awareness.

Each activity also offers a list of skills your child will learn, a list of minimal materials required, step-by-step directions that are easy to follow, additional ways to have even more fun, and advice to make sure your child stays safe during playtime.

Finally, you'll find resources at the back of the book that offer more information to help your kids keep busy and stay smart all summer long. You need not hear those cries of "I'm bored!" this summer. Your kids will have plenty to keep them busy, keep up their skills, and keep everybody happy.

You'd better get started now. Summer will be over before you know it!

# 1
# Animal Adventures

Snail Race

Buddy's Bowl

Bug Detective

Bug House

Pet Play

Spider Web Art

Tales of Super Pet

# Snail Race

Ages 3 to 9

Most racers are supposed to go fast when they race. So what happens when the racers are practically the slowest moving critters on the planet?

## Materials
★ Snails from the yard
★ Nontoxic colored markers or poster paints
★ Chalk

## Skills Learned
✔ Study of nature
✔ Understanding cause and effect
✔ Observation skills
✔ Creative and imaginative thinking

## What to Do
1. Find some snails in the yard, one for each player. Handle them carefully so they aren't hurt.
2. Color the snails' shells with markers or poster paint to make them unique and personal.
3. Draw a small racetrack with the chalk. Include a starting line and a finish line, with individual lanes for each snail.
4. Line up the snails at the starting line.
5. On the word "Go!" set the snails on the line and cheer them through their race to the finish line.

### Safety Tip
You don't want to upset the ecology, so be sure to return the snails to their original homes.

**6.** If a snail goes off its track, steer it (or carefully lift it) back on.

**7.** After you have a winner, return the snails back to their habitat.

# Buddy's Bowl

Ages 3 to 12

Jazz up mealtime for your favorite cat or dog by decorating your pet's food bowl.

## Materials

★ Dog or cat bowl
★ Acrylic paints or puffy paints
★ Paintbrush

## Skills Learned

✔ Fine motor development
✔ Creative and imaginative thinking
✔ Cognitive skills

## What to Do

**1.** Buy a pet dish or thoroughly wash the one your pet has been using.

**2.** Think about what kind of design you want to paint on the dish.

**3.** Paint your pet's name on the outside of the bowl first using fancy or creative letters.

**4.** Add decorations, animal faces, dots, stars, or other designs on the outside of the bowl with the paints.

### More Fun

Make a pet placemat to go under the bowl, using vinyl fabric and paints.

**5.** When the paint is dry, fill the bowl with pet food and invite your pet to dinner.

# Bug Detective

Ages 7 to 12

It takes an observant Bug Detective to search the plants, bushes, and other foliage for all the little critters that are creeping around the yard. How many can you find?

## Materials

★ Bug identification book
★ Magnifying glass
★ Colored pencils
★ Pad of paper

## Skills Learned

✔ Reading practice
✔ Writing skills
✔ Classification skills
✔ Study of natural environment and insect life
✔ Understanding scientific properties
✔ Math skills

## What to Do

1. Get a bug identification book from the library or bookstore.
2. Go out in the yard or to the park with your magnifying glass, pencils, and paper.
3. Using your detecting skills, look closely under rocks, leaves, and dirt for insects such as a ladybug, caterpillar, beetle, potato bug, earwig, ant, or worm.
4. When you find an insect, use your magnifying glass to study it carefully for a few minutes.
5. Draw a picture of the insect using the colored pencils.
6. Write about the insect's behavior or anything else that's interesting about the bug.
7. See how many insects you can find and record, then read about them in your bug book.
8. Check each day to see if you can discover more insects for your records.

### Safety Tip

Be careful not to study bumblebees and yellow jackets up close, or you might get stung!

# Bug House

Ages 7 to 12

Create a house or even a village for your backyard ants, bugs, or other critters.

## Materials

★ Small boxes, cans, sticks, or other objects to use as a foundation
★ Tape
★ Trowel, large old spoon, or other digging tool
★ Colored markers
★ Paper and pencil

## Skills Learned

✔ Planning and completing plans
✔ Cognitive skills/problem solving
✔ Classification skills
✔ Creative and imaginative thinking
✔ Study of nature
✔ Writing and recording skills

## What to Do

1. Find an area in the backyard with weeds, plants, and dirt.
2. Watch the area for a while to see what kinds of bug life you can find.
3. After you've studied the area, build a house or village for the critters using the materials listed above.
4. Decorate the house with colored markers or other decorations, if you like.
5. Carve out an area in the dirt and set the house there.
6. Watch how the bugs react to the new structure.
7. Record the activity of the bugs and how they respond to the house.

## More Fun

Create a playground for the bugs to crawl around by placing rocks, sticks, and other objects around the area. See what they do when they reach an obstacle.

# Pet Play

Ages 7 to 12

Have fun with your cat or dog and show him how much you care by playing some entertaining animal games each day.

## Materials

**Where's the Mouse? Cat Toy**
- ★ Large juice can or other can
- ★ 3-foot length of string
- ★ Small sock, rolled and tucked into a ball

**Go Get It! Dog Toy**
- ★ Newspaper or rubber bone
- ★ 4 to 6 feet of sturdy string

## Skills Learned

- ✔ Planning and completing plans
- ✔ Cognitive skills/problem solving
- ✔ Gross and fine motor development
- ✔ Social interaction

## What to Do

**Where's the Mouse? Cat Toy**
1. Open both ends of a juice can.
2. Tie a string around a small balled sock.
3. Drop the sock through the juice can, then lay the can on its side, leaving the sock several inches out.
4. Slowly pull the string so the sock disappears into the can.
5. See how your cat reacts.
6. Repeat until your cat gets tired of the game.

### Go Get It! Dog Toy

1. Roll up a newspaper or get a rubber bone and tie one end with sturdy string.
2. Hide yourself behind a bush or chair and toss the paper or bone in the middle of the yard or room in front of your dog.
3. Pull on the string just as your dog is about to retrieve it.
4. See how your dog reacts.
5. Repeat until your dog gets tired of the game.

**Safety Tip**

Don't tease your pet while you play; otherwise, he may get frustrated and bite you or learn not to trust you after a while.

# Spider Web Art

Ages 7 to 12

Take a picture from nature—without using a camera—by capturing a spider's work of art.

## Materials

★ Black construction paper
★ White spray paint
★ Spider web

## Skills Learned

✔ Study of nature
✔ Creative and imaginative thinking
✔ Geometric design

### What to Do

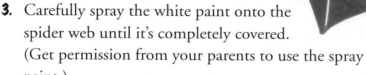

1. Get a sheet of black construction paper and some white spray paint.
2. Head for the yard and search the bushes, trees, and plants until you find a large spider web *without a spider.*
3. Carefully spray the white paint onto the spider web until it's completely covered. (Get permission from your parents to use the spray paint.)
4. Carefully press the black paper onto the spider web to capture the spray-painted web on paper.
5. Admire your spider web art.

### More Fun

See what other objects from nature you can capture. Try to make your own spider web using string. Create a spider out of a black pom-pom and pipe cleaners and add it to the design.

# Tales of Super Pet

Ages 7 to 12

Turn your pet into a super hero. Then have him use his special traits to save the world—or at least the neighborhood.

## Materials

★ Pet
★ Paper and pencil

## Skills Learned

✔ Observation skills
✔ Animal behavior
✔ Writing and creative expression

## What to Do

1. Study your pet for awhile and write down everything you see him do. Note the following:
   - His behavior
   - The sounds he makes
   - The expression in his eyes
   - His body language
   - The way he eats
   - How he reacts to you
   - Signs of various emotions, such as happiness, fear, anger, and so on

2. After you've taken notes based on your studies, write a story that features your pet as "Super Pet!"

3. Give your pet special powers based on some of his unique traits, such as "Super Smell," "Power Paws," "Flying Fur," and so on.

4. Continue writing a series of stories featuring your pet in different adventures. Put them together in a book.

### More Fun

Add illustrations to your stories and share them with your family and friends.
Have a friend write a story about his pet, then put both pets in the same story.

# 2
# Bookworm Fun

Crazy Cliffhangers
Library Time
Snack Story
Funny Pages
Mapping The Story
Rappin' Rhyme
Rewrite!
Bookmark It!
Storybook Soup
Tabloid News

# Crazy Cliffhangers

Ages 3 to 12

Here's a crazy way to give your favorite books a new twist. Can you guess what's going to happen next?

## Materials
★ Book with short chapters, comic book, or book of short stories
★ Paper and pencil

## Skills Learned
✔ Reading and language skills
✔ Creative and imaginative thinking
✔ Cognitive skills

## What to Do
1. Find a book from the library that looks interesting (or use our suggested booklist).
2. Read the first chapter.
3. Using your paper and pencil, write down what you think is going to happen next.
4. Read the next chapter and see if you're right.
5. Repeat for each chapter.
6. If you wrote something different from what happens in the book, put those pages together to form your own new book.

### More Fun
Read the first chapter of a short book, then read the second chapter of a different book, and so on. See what kind of crazy story you end up with.

# Library Time

Ages 3 to 12

Set aside once a week for Family Library Time, then bring home all the books you can hold for some reading fun.

## Materials
* ★ Library books
* ★ Paper and pencil

## Skills Learned
* ✔ Reading and vocabulary skills
* ✔ Family relationships
* ✔ Creative and imaginative thinking

## What to Do
1. Gather the family and head for the library.
2. Choose some books to take home that look interesting (or see our booklist).
3. When you're finished with a book, do one of the following:

   Make a Book Chart and list the titles of the books you read. Post your list on the wall and have your family members and friends keep their own lists. See who reads the most books during the summer.

   Have a book discussion night with your family and talk about what you liked and didn't like about the books you read. Mention what you would have done to make the book better.

If your parent reads the book to you, quiz each other on what happened in the latest chapter and see who can remember the most details.

Retell the story to each other, taking turns, but contribute parts of your own stories to the storytelling so you end up with a wild new story.

See if you can tell the story backwards.

## More Fun

Read your book to your family and ask them to guess what's going to happen next in the story.

# Snack Story

Ages 3 to 12

It's easy to write a story with pencil and paper. But can you write without them?

## Materials

★ Alphabet cereal, alphabet noodles, or alphabet cookies
★ Construction paper
★ Glue

## Skills Learned

✔ Writing and language development
✔ Creative and imaginative thinking
✔ Cognitive skills

## Safety Tip

Make sure the alphabet letters are edible before you eat them. And don't eat them after they're glued onto the paper!

## What to Do

1. Buy alphabet cereal, noodles, or cookies (or all three if you're hungry!).
2. Think of a story or letter you want to write.
3. Write the story with the alphabet letters by gluing them onto the paper.
4. When you finish the story, eat the leftovers.

# Funny Pages

Ages 7 to 12

To find out if you have a funny bone, write a few words in some speech balloons and make your own comic strip.

## Materials

★ Large sheet of paper
★ Sunday funny papers
★ Scissors, glue, or tape
★ White-out
★ Fine-tip markers

## Skills Learned

✔ Creative writing and expression
✔ Sense of humor
✔ Logic and sequencing
✔ Cognitive skills

## What to Do

1. Cut out a variety of panels from the funny papers.
2. Cut them into individual squares.
3. Cut off or white-out the words in the speech balloons.
4. Arrange the squares on the large sheet of paper and glue or tape them in a row to make a new strip.
5. Write your own words in the speech balloons to create a new comic strip.
6. Make your own comic book using several sheets of comic strips.

### More Fun

Draw your own cartoon characters and speech balloons to create a brand new comic strip.

# Mapping the Story

Ages 7 to 12

If you really want to put yourself into the story, draw a map to keep track of where you've been.

## Materials

★ Good book
★ Paper and pencil
★ Large sheet of paper
★ Colored markers
★ Ruler (optional)

## Skills Learned

✔ Reading comprehension
✔ Mapping skills
✔ Logical thinking
✔ Creative and imaginative thinking

## What to Do

1. Choose a book from the recommended reading list or borrow a book that a friend recommends.

2. As you read the story, make notes about the location of the story, such as the name of the town or street, buildings mentioned, places the character visits, and so on.

3. Each time you finish a chapter, use your notes to draw a map showing the places mentioned in the story.

4. As you read more of the story, add to your map any new streets, buildings, and sites that are mentioned.

5. When the story is finished, fill in the details, then hang your map on your wall. If you borrowed the book from a friend, show him your map and see if he recognizes the sites from the story.

### More Fun

Draw paper dolls of the main characters and cut them out. Set them on the map as you follow the story. When the story is finished, use the map to create a new adventure for the characters.

# Rappin' Rhyme

### Ages 7 to 12

Make up your own rhymes or update favorite old songs and rap them to your friends and family.

## Materials

★ Book of rhymes and poems
★ Paper and pencil
★ Cassette player and tape
★ Musical tapes (optional)

## Skills Learned

✔ Writing and language skills
✔ Memory development
✔ Creative and imaginative thinking
✔ Rhythm and music appreciation
✔ Self-confidence

## What to Do

1. Find a book of poems or rhymes from the library or bookstore and choose a few favorites.
2. Rewrite the poems or rhymes to modernize them, personalize them, and make them humorous.
3. Then try writing your own funny poems and rhymes.
4. When your poem is finished, say it out loud to a rapping beat.
5. Repeat it a few times until you've memorized the rap and then perform it for friends or family members.

### More Fun

Rap your poem on a cassette recorder and create a dance step to go with your rap.

# Rewrite!

Ages 7 to 12

Write your own funny story using an old favorite as a guide. It's as easy as filling in the blanks.

## Materials

★ Favorite short story
★ Pencil
★ White-out

## Skills Learned

✔ Writing and storytelling
✔ Language and vocabulary
✔ Creative and imaginative thinking
✔ Social interaction

## What to Do

1. Find a short story in a magazine, such as *Ranger Rick, Nickelodeon, American Girl,* or other source.
2. With a pencil, underline some of the nouns (person, place, or thing), verbs (action words, such as "run," "scream," or "fell"), adjectives (words that describe the nouns, such as "beautiful," "large," or "blue"), and adverbs (words used with verbs that end in "ly," such as "quickly," "quietly," or "shyly").
3. Underneath the underlined words, write down what kind of word it is—noun, verb, adjective, or adverb.

## Safety Tip

Be careful with the white-out—it doesn't come off your clothes or furniture easily.

**4.** White-out the underlined words so you can't read them anymore (but don't white-out the identifying words underneath).

**5.** Ask a friend to replace the missing words by having her say a noun where a noun used to be, a verb where a verb used to be, and so on. Encourage your friend to be creative with the new words. For example, if you need a noun, your friend might say "pig," "hamburger," or "mud puddle." If you need a verb, your friend might say "wiggle," "belch," or "play."

**6.** Write the new words in the white space on the line using black marker, or make new speech balloons and paste them over the others.

**7.** When all the spaces are filled in, read the story out loud and see how funny it turns out.

**8.** Take turns rewriting the stories and reading them out loud.

# Bookmark It!

Ages 7 to 12

Make these magical bookmarks for all your books—
and then for all your friends' and family's books.

## Materials

★ Posterboard or stiff cardstock paper
★ Ruler and pencil
★ Decorative paper, such as
wrapping paper, comic
strips, or comic books, or
inexpensive illustrated books
★ Colorful markers
★ Glitter, stickers, ribbon,
decals
★ Scissors
★ Glue
★ Peel-and-stick magnetic
tape (available at the drug-
store or hardware store)

## Skills Learned

✔ Following instructions
✔ Fine motor development
✔ Creative and imaginative
thinking
✔ Measuring

## What to Do

1. Use a ruler to measure a rectangular strip of posterboard
   or cardstock about 2 inches wide by 6 inches long. Cut
   out the strip. (Make as many strips as you like!)
2. Carefully fold the strip in half so each half is about
   2 inches by 3 inches.

3. Decorate the outside of the front and back of the bookmark in one of the following ways:

Unfold the bookmark and cover it with decorative paper by cutting wrapping paper the same size as the bookmark, spreading a thin layer of glue on the top side of the strip, and covering it with the paper.

Keep the bookmark folded and glue cartoon characters or illustrated book characters on either side (make sure the heads are up toward the folded end).

Use the colored markers to draw the front of a favorite character (such as Anne of Green Gables or Charlotte from *Charlotte's Web*) on one side of the folded bookmark and the character's back side on the other side of the bookmark (head toward the fold).

Decorate the bookmark with glitter, sequins, stickers, ribbon, decals, or whatever you like by gluing or sticking them onto the outside of the bookmark.

4. Keep the bookmark folded and allow the decorations or drawings to dry.

5. Cut two small squares off the magnetic tape.

6. Remove the paper backing from one piece of magnetic tape and stick

## More Fun

Make Crittermarks by cutting strips of felt 2 inches by 6 inches, then gluing on a pom-pom at the top to make the animal's head, gluing on wiggly eyes, then adding a face and body details with bits of felt. Cut a strip of felt for the tail, glue it to the bottom, and then allow it to dry. Insert your Crittermark between the last and next-to-last pages of your book, making sure the critter's head is sticking out at the top. Or make Nature Bookmarks by sticking a flower or leaf on clear Con-Tact paper then folding it over and cutting it out.

it on the inside of the folded bookmark at the end (not at the fold).

7. Stick the other piece of the magnetic tape to the other end so that when the bookmark is folded in half, the two magnetic pieces stick together. Check to make sure your magnet pieces attract each other before you secure them.

8. Read a chapter in a book and then mark your place by folding the magnetic bookmark over the next page so that when you return to the book, you can find your place easily.

# Storybook Soup

Ages 7 to 12

If you like to make up stories but sometimes get stuck, try "borrowing" a few friends from your favorite storybooks to help you out.

## Materials
★ 2 or 3 favorite storybooks
★ Paper and pencil

## Skills Learned
✔ Creative writing and language
✔ Reading and vocabulary
✔ Creative and imaginative thinking
✔ Self-expression

## What to Do

1. Reread 2 or 3 of your favorite storybooks, or read some new ones, if you like.

2. As you read, jot down the names of the main characters and note some of their interesting characteristics, such as "Anne is strong-willed," and "Peter acts like a kid."

3. Also, as you read, jot down two or three plot points. Plot points are unexpected developments in a story that surprise you and turn the story in a new direction. For example, Anne of Green Gables is adopted by a gruff couple when her parents die, and Peter Pan has to walk a pirate ship plank.

4. Combine the two characters into a brand new story using ideas from the two plot points. For example, Anne and Peter are adopted by pirates, but just as they walk the plank, they discover they have magical powers.

5. Let the characters' interaction create the story while you add more plot points—problems for the characters to solve. Let each character contribute to the solution in his or her unique way.

6. When the story is finished, give it a creative title, such as "Escape from Pirate Island" or "Anne and Her Magical Friends."

7. Share the story with your friends and family.

### More Fun

If you do this with a friend, have everyone choose the same three characters and plot points and then write their own stories. Even though the story elements are the same, you'll be surprised how differently each story turns out.

# Tabloid News

Ages 7 to 12

Make up some ridiculous and exaggerated news and see how wild you can make the headlines.

## Materials

★ Tabloid newspaper, optional
★ Magazines
★ Scissors
★ Glue
★ Paper and pencil

## Skills Learned

✔ Writing and language development
✔ Reading skills
✔ Creative and imaginative thinking
✔ Cognitive skills

## What to Do

1. If you like, read over a tabloid newspaper to get the feeling for this type of wild, sensational news.
2. Go through some old magazines and cut out a few interesting pictures.
3. Glue the pictures on a sheet of paper, leaving room to write headlines and short articles.
4. Think up some wild headlines and crazy stories to go with the pictures. For example, if you choose an advertisement for headache medicine that features a person who looks like

### More Fun

Instead of using magazine pictures, take snapshots of your friends and family making funny faces or doing wild poses, then use these for your Tabloid News.

she's in pain, you might write a headline such as "ALIENS STOLE MY BRAIN!" or "MY TEACHER ATE MY HOMEWORK!" Then write a story to go with the picture and your headline.

# 3
# Brain Busters

ONCE UPON A TIME THERE WAS A [gingerbread man] WHO HAD NO [shoes] SO HE USED HIS [cell phone] TO CALL A [grasshopper] FOR A RIDE.

**Watch the Marble**

**Good News, Bad News**

**Dicey Stories**

**Letter Puzzle**

**Mirror Writing**

**Rebus Writing**

# Watch the Marble

Ages 3 to 9

If you've got fast hands, you'll astound your friends and family with this simple but amazing trick.

## Materials

★ 2 to 3 whole walnuts with shells
★ Nutcracker
★ Marble

## Skills Learned

✔ Cognitive development/ problem solving
✔ Social skills
✔ Fine and gross motor development/coordination
✔ Competence/self-esteem

## What to Do

1. Carefully crack open the walnuts and remove the nut meat. (Feel free to eat the meat!)
2. Choose the three best-looking half shells for the trick. They should have smooth edges so they'll slide easily.
3. Place the 3 shells face down on a table.
4. Put a marble under one of the shells.
5. Mix up the shells by moving them around,

### More Fun

If you really want to fool them, here's another trick. As you move the shells around, allow the shell holding the marble to move slightly over the edge of the table so the marble secretly drops down into your lap. That way, no matter which marble your friend picks, he'll never get it right because the marble is in your lap.

weaving them in between each other several times, as rapidly as you can.

6. See if you can guess where the marble is.

7. When you get good at moving the shells and fooling yourself, try it on your friends and see if they can tell where the marble is.

# Good News, Bad News

Ages 3 to 12

Are you an optimist or a pessimist? Find out when you have a Good News, Bad News conversation with a friend.

## Materials
★ Paper and pencil (optional)

## Skills Learned
✔ Creative and imaginative thinking
✔ Cognitive skills
✔ Problem solving
✔ Language development
✔ Social interaction
✔ Positive attitude

## What to Do
1. Find a pal to chat with and decide who will be the optimist (the person who looks at the positive side of life) and who will be the pessimist (the person who looks at the negative side of life).

2. Pick a topic to discuss, such as "Summer Vacation," "Back to School," "That New Teacher," "Getting a Dog," and so on.

3. The optimist starts the conversation by saying something positive about the topic. For example, if the topic is "Summer Vacation," he might say, "I love summer because it's so long!"

4. The pessimist must reply to the optimist's statement by saying something negative, such as, "But summer is so long that I get really bored!"

5. The optimist and the pessimist keep taking turns until one player can't think of anything else to say.

6. The last person to give a response gets a point.

7. Start another conversation with a new topic, but this time trade roles so that the optimist is the pessimist this time and the pessimist is the optimist! Try not to get mixed up.

## More Fun

When you get tired of "Good News, Bad News," play "Could Be Worse!" One player begins by making a statement, such as, "I have to go to the doctor today." The other player must say something worse than that, such as, "Could be worse—you could be going to the dentist." Take turns as you continue making the situation worse and worse by exaggerating more and more, such as, "Could be worse—I could be getting a cavity filled!" "Could be worse—you could be getting a tooth pulled!"

# Dicey Stories

Ages 7 to 12

You'll have to think fast when the dice roll or you may be at a loss for words.

## Materials

★ Dictionary or list of spelling words
★ Pair of dice
★ Paper with adhesive backing
★ Pen
★ Scissors
★ Stopwatch or watch with a second hand

## Skills Learned

✔ Vocabulary and language development
✔ Cognitive skills/quick thinking
✔ Social interaction

## What to Do

1. Find 12 interesting words in the dictionary or use your spelling words.
2. Make sure you know the meaning of each word.
3. Write the words on a sheet of adhesive paper, small enough to fit on one side of a single die (two make a pair

the red bird landed on my dog's nose.

of dice), or use two toy blocks, which might be easier since they're larger.

4. Cut out the words and stick them onto the dice so that all the sides have a word.

5. The first player rolls the dice, while another player keeps track of the time.

6. That player has 30 seconds to come up with a sentence using both words on the top of the dice.

7. When the person timing calls "Stop!" after 30 seconds, the next player rolls the dice and must come up with a sentence using both the words on the top of the dice—and the sentence must connect to the previous sentence.

8. Keep taking turns rolling the dice, keeping time, and making up sentences using the two words on the top of the dice to continue the story.

## More Fun

Instead of writing words on the dice, play with one die and begin a story using only the number on the top of the die. For example, if you roll a "5," you may only use 5 words, such as, "There was an old witch." Continue taking turns rolling the die and continuing the story with the number of words required. If you roll a "3" next, you might add, "She was ugly!"

# Letter Puzzle

Ages 7 to 12

You know the alphabet forwards and backwards, but how many words can you make from all those letters?

## Materials

★ Sheet of paper
★ Colored markers
★ Magazine or newspaper
★ Glue

## Skills Learned

✔ Spelling and vocabulary
✔ Cognitive skills
✔ Spatial relationships

## What to Do

1. Draw a grid on a large sheet of paper and make 10 squares across by 10 squares down, so you have a total of 100 squares.
2. Cut 100 letters out of a magazine or newspaper to fit inside the squares.
3. Mix up the letters and place them onto the squares until the grid is completely filled with letters.
4. See how many words you can make by connecting the letters, in any direction, and write them on a separate piece of paper. The letters must be next to each other, and you can use the same letter more than once.
5. Circle the words you find with a colored marker.
6. Count how many words you find.
7. Make another grid and see if you can find even more words.

### More Fun

Photocopy the grid of letters, or write on a separate sheet of paper, give it to a friend, and see who can find the most words in a limited period of time.

# Mirror Writing

Ages 7 to 12

You've been writing your name so long you could probably write it blindfolded. But can you write it in the mirror?

## Materials
★ Several sheets of blank paper
★ Pencil or pen
★ Hand mirror

## Skills Learned
✔ Fine motor control/ handwriting
✔ Eye-hand coordination
✔ Cognitive skills/problem solving
✔ Spatial perception

## What to Do
1. Write your name on the paper.
2. Set the paper on the table, opposite the mirror, so you can see the paper in the mirror's reflection.
3. Try to trace over your name, looking *only* in the mirror, not directly at the paper. See how difficult it is to just trace your own handwriting from a mirror image.
4. Write your name again by looking only in the mirror this time and without tracing.
5. See if you can write your name backwards so that it comes out forwards and looks like your normal handwriting.

## More Fun
Try drawing other pictures using the mirror and see how well you do.

# Rebus Writing

Ages 7 to 12

They say a "picture's worth a thousand words," but can a picture be worth only one word?

## Materials
★ Magazines
★ Paper and pencil
★ Glue or tape

## Skills Learned
✔ Writing and vocabulary
✔ Fine motor skills
✔ Creative and imaginative thinking
✔ Visual and cognitive development

## What to Do
1. Cut out some small interesting pictures from magazines.
2. Arrange the pictures on a table so you can see them clearly.
3. Choose a picture to start your story.
4. Write the first line of the story, incorporating the selected picture in the sentence, and actually use the picture to replace the word. For example, if you have

a picture of a dinosaur, you might begin your story like this: "Once upon a time there was a big purple dinosaur." But instead of writing the words "purple dinosaur," glue the picture where the words would be.

5. Choose another picture and continue the story with another sentence, writing the words but inserting the picture when appropriate.

6. Try to use all the pictures you've selected as you tell your story.

> ## More Fun
>
> For a real challenge, glue the pictures on the paper first, placing them randomly over the page. Then write the story to fit the order of the pictures.

7. End the story when you get to the last picture.

8. Now share your Rebus story with a friend or family member and see if they can read the story with the pictures substituted for words.

# 4
# Chill Out

Summer Snowstorm

Upside-Down Sundaes

Frozen Slushies

Fruit Juice Pops

Frozen Fun

Banana Smoothie

Egg Cream

Fan It

Ice Cream in a Can

Ice Creamwich

Ice Sculpture

# Summer Snowstorm

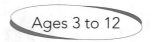

Ages 3 to 12

A snowstorm in the middle of the summer? Yes, it's possible—if you make your own "snowballs."

## Materials
★ Vanilla ice cream
★ Plate
★ Ice cream scoop or large rounded spoon
★ 1 cup flaked coconut

## Skills Learned
✔ Reading and following directions
✔ Creative and imaginative thinking
✔ Fine motor skills

## What to Do
1. Soften the ice cream by setting it on the counter a few minutes.
2. Pour some coconut into a plate.
3. Scoop out a round ball of ice cream.
4. Roll the ice cream ball in coconut.
5. Place the ball in the freezer to firm up.
6. Make as many snowballs as you like.
7. When the balls are firm, stack them in a pile and serve them to your hot and hungry friends and family.

## More Fun
Make colored snowballs by buying ice cream, frozen yogurt, or sherbet in a variety of colors, then tint the coconut to match by shaking it in a plastic bag with a few drops of food coloring. Make a snowman by stacking 3 snowballs of different sizes, then adding features with tubes of frosting or decorative candies.

# Upside-Down Sundaes

Ages 3 to 12

Have some upside-down fun in the sun with these Up-side-Down Sundaes. Just don't eat them upside-down!

## Materials
★ Small clear bowl or cup
★ 1 cherry
★ 1 tablespoon whipped cream
★ 1 tablespoon chopped nuts or sprinkles
★ 2 to 3 tablespoons choco-late or caramel syrup
★ 1 to 2 scoops of your fa-vorite ice cream or frozen yogurt

## Skills Learned
✔ Reading and following directions
✔ Creative and imaginative thinking
✔ Math and measurement
✔ Fine motor development

## What to Do
1. Place the cherry at the bottom of a bowl or cup.
2. Scoop or spray a layer of whipped cream.
3. Sprinkle with chopped nuts or sprinkles.
4. Drizzle on chocolate or caramel syrup.

5. Top with 1 to 2 scoops of ice cream or frozen yogurt.
6. Eat your Upside-Down Sundae—with an upside-down spoon.

## More Fun

Instead of making an upside-down sundae, make an ice cream parfait by layering the ingredients in a tall clear glass. Be creative and see what interesting ingredients you can come up with.

# Frozen Slushies

Ages 3 to 12

Tingle your tongue with an icy cold slushy made from your favorite fruit juice.

## Materials
★ Paper cups
★ Fruit juice
★ Fork
★ Plastic spoons

## Skills Learned
✔ Math and measuring
✔ Understanding scientific properties
✔ Fine motor skills
✔ Following directions

## What to Do
1. Fill the paper cups with fruit juice.
2. Place in the freezer for 2 hours.

3. Remove from the freezer and stab the frozen fruit juice with a fork to break it up.

4. Stir and return the slushy to the freezer for another ½ hour.

5. Remove, stab, and stir again, then serve with a spoon.

**More Fun**

Freeze fruit, such as grapes, raspberries, strawberries, or bananas, until firm. Whirl in the blender with a little juice and some ice cubes until slushy, then pour into cups.

# Fruit Juice Pops

Ages 3 to 12

It's easy and fun to make your own Popsicles—and you can make them just the way you like.

## Materials

★ Fruit juice, such as orange juice, cranberry juice, lemonade, grapefruit juice, or grape juice
★ Popsicle molds or paper cups and Popsicle sticks or ice-cube trays

## Skills Learned

✔ Cause and effect
✔ Math and measurement
✔ Understanding scientific properties
✔ Good nutrition

## What to Do

1. Buy a bottle of your favorite fruit juice, or mix up juice from frozen concentrate, following the directions on the can.

**2.** Pour the juice into the molds or paper cups or ice-cube trays. If you use paper cups, cover the tops with foil and insert Popsicle sticks in the center. If you use ice trays, lay Popsicle sticks in each compartment.

**3.** Place the molds in the freezer until firm, 4 to 6 hours or overnight.

**4.** Release the pops from the mold by holding the bottom under running water.

**5.** Enjoy your Fruit Juice Pops.

## More Fun

Add a piece of fruit to each pop. Layer different fruit juices in the molds to make rainbow pops. Think of other containers you can use for molding the pops, such as gelatin molds, bowls, and so on. Chop up your pop and turn them into slushies.

# Frozen Fun

Ages 7 to 12

When it's hot outside, you can chill out inside with lots of creative frosty treats. What else can you turn into Frozen Fun?

## Materials

### Fruit Surprise

★ Ice-cube tray
★ Fruit juice
★ Cherries, pineapple bites, grapes, strawberries

### Arctic Oranges

★ Oranges
★ Frozen vanilla yogurt

### Banana Pops

★ Bananas
★ Popsicle sticks
★ Coconut, peanut butter, chocolate

### Watermelon Wedgies

★ Watermelon
★ Popsicle sticks

## Skills Learned

✔ Creative thinking
✔ Understanding scientific properties
✔ Cognitive skills/cause and effect

## What to Do

### Fruit Surprise

1. Put a piece of fruit in each ice-cube tray compartment.
2. Fill the tray with fruit juice.
3. Freeze until firm.
4. Pop out individual cubes into small paper cups and enjoy.

### Arctic Oranges

1. Cut the tops off oranges.
2. Scoop out orange and place in a small bowl.
3. Squeeze out juice.

4. Soften yogurt and mix with orange juice.
5. Refill hollow orange rinds and freeze until firm.
6. Serve with spoons.

### Banana Pops

1. Peel bananas and cut in half.
2. Insert Popsicle sticks into the flat end of the sliced bananas.
3. Roll bananas in peanut butter and coconut or melted chocolate.
4. Lay on waxed paper and freeze until firm.
5. Remove from paper and enjoy.

### Safety Tips

★ Check with parents before freezing something, in case it's a food that might explode when frozen!
★ Have your parents handle the knives, or handle them carefully, if you're allowed to use them.

### Watermelon Wedgies

1. Cut watermelon into wedges the size of your palm, about 2 inches thick.
2. Insert Popsicle sticks into wedges.
3. Freeze until firm, then enjoy.

# Banana Smoothie

### Ages 7 to 12

Turn a banana into a smooth and refreshing drink—then try some other fruit smoothies using different ingredients.

## Materials

* ★ 1½ cups lowfat milk
* ★ 1 large banana
* ★ 1 scoop lowfat vanilla ice cream
* ★ ¼ teaspoon vanilla
* ★ Blender
* ★ Glass

## Skills Learned

* ✔ Reading and following directions
* ✔ Cognitive skills/ classification
* ✔ Cause and effect
* ✔ Good nutrition
* ✔ Independence/competence

## What to Do

1. Pour milk into the blender.
2. Peel a banana, break it into several pieces, and put it in the blender.
3. Add ice cream and vanilla.
4. Cover the top of the blender and whirl on medium speed until smooth. Stop the blender and stir after a few seconds if the ingredients aren't mixing.
5. Pour into glasses and enjoy your refreshing drink with a straw or a spoon.

## Safety Tips

* ★ Get your parent's supervision when using the blender.
* ★ Remember to keep the lid on while you're blending, or the mixture may go all over the room!

# Egg Cream

Ages 7 to 12

Entertain your friends with this classic New York soda that's not even made out of eggs or cream. So how did it get its name? Good question!

## Materials

★ 1 cup club soda or fizzy water
★ 1 cup milk
★ 1 tablespoon chocolate syrup
★ Pitcher
★ 2 tall glasses

## Skills Learned

✔ Reading and following directions
✔ Cognitive skills
✔ Scientific properties/ cause and effect
✔ Math and measurement

## What to Do

1. Pour club soda into a tall, wide pitcher.
2. Add milk and chocolate syrup and stir rapidly—or use a wire whisk, an egg beater, or the blender to mix the ingredients.
3. Set the 2 tall glasses on the table.
4. Carefully stand on a chair with the pitcher.
5. Carefully pour the Egg Cream into the 2 glasses. (You might want to practice this a few times before you show off your pouring skills.)
6. Clean up any spills you make, then enjoy your authentic Egg Cream— with no egg or cream!

## More Fun

Use chocolate milk if you prefer, to make the drink extra chocolaty.

# Fan It

Ages 7 to 12

Here's one way to keep cool on those hot days. Make a fan and blow up a cool breeze.

## Materials
★ Construction paper
★ Colorful markers
★ Stapler
★ Tongue depressor
★ Tape

## Skills Learned
✔ Following directions
✔ Problem solving/cause and effect
✔ Understanding scientific properties
✔ Cognitive skills

## How to Play
1. Fold a sheet of construction paper back and forth like an accordion.
2. Press the folds firmly so they'll be stiff.
3. Unfold the paper.
4. Draw a picture or write a message using *every other* space.
5. Refold the paper and staple it at the bottom.
6. Securely tape a tongue depressor to the bottom to make a handle.
7. Hold the fan at the bottom, allowing it to slightly unfold.

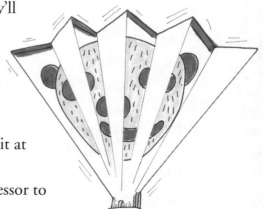

**8.** Watch the picture reveal itself in the folds.

**9.** Fan yourself to keep cool as you enjoy your picture.

## More Fun

Draw another picture or write something else on the blank spaces, too, so that when you look at the fan from one side you see one picture, and when you look at it from the other side you see a different picture.

# Ice Cream in a Can

Ages 7 to 12

Surprisingly, you can make your own ice cream using a plain old coffee can. Just fill the can, roll it around, and eat the ice cream!

## Materials

★ 2 empty coffee cans, one about 12 ounces and one a little larger, with lids
★ 1 cup heavy cream
★ 1 cup nonfat milk
★ 1 beaten egg
★ ⅓ cup sugar
★ 1 teaspoon vanilla
★ Crushed ice
★ Rock salt

## Skills Learned

✔ Reading and following directions
✔ Understanding scientific properties
✔ Math and measurement
✔ Fine and gross motor skills
✔ Cause and effect
✔ Social interaction

## What to Do

1. Clean out the coffee cans.
2. Combine cream, milk, egg, sugar, and vanilla in the smaller coffee can and close the lid.
3. Set the smaller can in the large can.
4. Fill the space between the cans with layers of crushed ice and rock salt and then close the lid.
5. Sit on the ground opposite a friend and roll the can back and forth for about 10 minutes.
6. Open the larger can and pour off the water, salt, and ice.
7. Open the smaller can and stir the contents, especially along the sides of the can.
8. Replace the lid and fill the space between the small and large can with more crushed ice and rock salt.
9. Replace the lid and roll another 5 to 10 minutes.
10. Check the contents again to see if the cream mixture has become ice cream. If not, pour off the water, salt, and ice again; stir the contents of the smaller can; fill the space with ice and salt; and continue to roll another 5 to 10 minutes.
11. When the ice cream is ready, scoop it out and serve immediately. Chopped fruit can be added to the finished ice cream to flavor it.

## Safety Tips

★ Be careful of any sharp edges on the coffee cans.
★ Give your arms a break so you don't get a muscle cramp!

# Ice Creamwich

Ages 7 to 12

You can make your own ice cream sandwiches in all sorts of flavors to cool down on a hot day.

## Materials
★ Large bakery or home-made cookies, such as chocolate chip, oatmeal, or peanut butter (2 for each sandwich)
★ Plate
★ Favorite ice cream flavor
★ Spoon and dull knife
★ Plastic wrap

## Skills Learned
✔ Reading and following directions
✔ Math and measurement
✔ Creative and imaginative thinking
✔ Understanding scientific properties

## What to Do
1. Set 2 cookies on a plate, flat side up.
2. Soften ice cream a little by setting it on the counter or putting it in the microwave for a few seconds.

## More Fun

Roll the sides of the Creamwich in a bowl of colorful sprinkles to make it more festive. Make and sell Creamwiches as a summer business (keep them inside the freezer so they won't melt). See how many different Creamwiches you can make using different cookies and ice cream flavors.

3. Scoop out a spoonful of ice cream and spread it onto one of the cookies, about ¾-inch thick. Smooth it with a knife.

4. Top with the other cookie and smooth the sides with the knife.

5. Wrap in plastic wrap and place in freezer for about 1 to 2 hours to firm it up.

6. Repeat for other cookies.

7. When they're ready to eat, unwrap Creamwiches and enjoy.

# Ice Sculpture

Ages 7 to 12

Working with ice should keep you cool for a while in the heat.

## Materials
★ Large bowl
★ Plastic bag
★ Food coloring
★ Small hammer
★ Butter knife or chisel
★ Glitter (optional)

## Skills Learned
✔ Fine motor skills
✔ Eye-hand coordination
✔ Creative and imaginative thinking
✔ Cause and effect

## What to Do
1. Fill a large bowl with water and place it in the freezer (or buy a large block of ice).

2. Freeze overnight until firm.

3. Turn out the chunk of ice by running warm water over the bottom of the bowl.

4. Set the ice on the garbage bag and take it outside to the lawn or picnic table in the shade.

5. Using a small hammer, chip away at the ice with the butter knife or chisel to create an interesting sculpture. Be careful with the hammer and knife or chisel so you don't slam your thumb or cut your finger!

6. Work quickly before the ice melts! Then keep the ice sculpture in the freezer until time to display the centerpiece.

## More Fun

Sprinkle with glitter when you're finished. Or add food coloring to the ice to make it colorful. Freeze water in a variety of interesting containers, such as a rubber glove or gelatin mold for added fun, and run water over the glove or mold to make it easy to release. Use eye droppers filled with food coloring to drip onto the ice and make the sculpture multicolored. Add a little salt and see what happens to the colored ice.

# 5
# Crafty Creations

**Magic Motion**

**Pressed Flowers**

**Slime and Oobleck**

**Veggie Monster**

**Pom-Pom Pets**

**Rainbow Scape**

**Scrapbook**

**Shoe Shiners**

# Magic Motion

Ages 3 to 12

Watch the images magically appear as you move your crayon back and forth like a magic wand.

## Materials

★ Flowers, leaves, grave-stones, petroglyphs, sea-shells, and other flat nature items
★ Newspapers
★ Thin white and colored paper
★ Tape
★ Crayons with paper peeled off

## Skills Learned

✔ Creative and imaginative thinking
✔ Cognitive skills/cause and effect
✔ Nature study

## What to Do

1. Find some interesting nature objects to use for your rub-bings, such as the objects mentioned above. Make sure they are somewhat flat so you can get a good image.
2. Lay a few sheets of newspaper on the table for padding.
3. Place an object on the newspaper, such as a flower or leaf.
4. Set a sheet of white paper over the objects and tape the paper to the newspaper or table so it won't slide around.
5. Choose a color crayon other than white and lay it flat on the paper.
6. Move the crayon slowly over the object and watch the image appear.

**7.** Lift the paper and move the objects to a different spot under the paper.

**8.** Replace the paper and move another crayon over the object until it appears. Repeat as much as you like.

**Safety Tips**

★ Get permission before you do a rubbing on a public or private image, such as a petroglyph or memorial.
★ Be careful you don't get crayon marks on the gravestones and other objects.

**9.** Try using different colors of paper with crayons in contrasting colors. Try black paper with a white crayon and see what happens.

# Pressed Flowers

Ages 3 to 12

Preserve a little bit of nature and turn it into a special gift or decoration, to bring some natural beauty indoors.

## Materials

★ Flowers or leaves
★ Thick book
★ Scissors
★ Burlap
★ Clear Con-Tact paper
★ Posterboard picture frame
★ Glue

## Skills Learned

✔ Nature studies
✔ Cognitive skills/cause and effect
✔ Creative and imaginative thinking

## What to Do

1. Look around the yard for an interesting flower or leaf.
2. Get permission before you pick any flowers or leaves, then select a few to preserve.
3. Open a thick book and place the flower or leaf flat on a page near the back. Arrange the object so it looks the way you want it when it's dry.
4. Carefully close the book, place something heavy on top of it, and let it sit for a few days.
5. In the meantime, prepare a placemat and picture frame to use with the pressed flowers or leaves.

   *For the placemat:* Cut burlap into approximately 10- by 12-inch rectangles. Fringe the ends by pulling off threads on all four sides. When the flowers are ready, arrange them on the mat the way you want them. Then cover the flowers and mat with clear Con-Tact paper the same size as the mat, leaving the fringe exposed.

   *For the picture frame:* Buy or make a frame by cutting 2 pieces of posterboard into a square or rectangle the same size. Cut a hole out of the center of one of the cardboard rectangles to display the picture. Glue a picture in the center of the plain rectangle and then place the cut-out rectangle on top, centering the hole over the picture. Glue the frame pieces together. Arrange flowers or leaves around the frame and glue them on. Cut out strips of clear Con-Tact paper and wrap the strips over the flowers and around the frame.

## Safety Tips

★ Don't pick any flowers or plants that don't belong to you unless you get permission.
★ Watch out for poison oak and ivy.
★ Be careful with the scissors.
★ Don't get the clear Con-Tact paper stuck all over you!

# Slime and Oobleck

Ages 3 to 12

Ready to get your hands dirty? You're about to be slimed—not to mention ooblecked, mooshed, and gooed.

## Materials

### Slime

★ 2 cups white glue
★ 1½ cups water
★ 1 cup water
★ 4 teaspoons borax

### Oobleck

★ 2 cups cornstarch
★ ½ cup water
★ Food coloring

### Dough

★ 4 cups flour
★ 1 cup salt
★ 1¾ cups water
★ Food coloring

### Goo

★ 2 to 3 packages fruit-flavored gelatin in colors that match or mix well with the food coloring.

## Skills Learned

✔ Cognitive skills
✔ Scientific properties
✔ Creative and imaginative thinking
✔ Cause and effect
✔ Fine motor development

## What to Do

### Slime

1. Combine 2 cups white glue and 1½ cups water in a medium bowl.
2. In a second bowl, mix 1 cup water and 4 teaspoons borax.
3. Combine the contents of both bowls together in one large bowl.
4. Watch what happens as you enjoy playing with the Slime.

### Oobleck

1. Combine 2 cups cornstarch with ½ cup water.
2. Add food coloring and mix well with your hands.
3. Feel the mixture change in your hands from dry to wet, hard to soft, firm to slimy, and white to colorful.
4. Enjoy squeezing and handling the Oobleck.

### Dough

1. Combine 4 cups flour, 1 cup salt, and 1¾ cups water in a large bowl.
2. Mix well with your hands.
3. Divide into separate small bowls and add a different food coloring to each bowl.
4. Mix well with your hands.
5. Make monsters, critters, or anything you like with the dough.
6. When you're finished making things, bake your creations for 1 to 2 hours at 250 degrees to harden it.
7. Paint it with shellac if you want to preserve it for a long time.

### Goo

1. Mix up 2 to 3 packages of gelatin in a mixing bowl, according to package directions.

2. Fill a pan with the mixture and allow it to set in the refrigerator until semi-firm.

3. Remove from refrigerator and turn out your mixture on a cookie sheet.

**Safety Tips**

★ Be careful not to get the slimy stuff on your clothes or furniture—it doesn't come off easily.
★ Don't taste anything but the gelatin (your goo). The rest is yucky.

4. Enjoy the goo (and feel free to lick your fingers as long as your hands are clean).

5. Firm up the goo by adding a package of unflavored gelatin for every package of fruit gelatin and then allow it to set completely. Cut it into shapes and play with your jigglers.

# Veggie Monster

Ages 3 to 12

You don't have to like vegetables to play with them. Just turn them into monsters and enjoy their company.

## Materials
★ Variety of vegetables, such as potato, bell pepper, zucchini, carrot, celery, cauliflower, broccoli, and so on
★ Sharp knife
★ Cutting board
★ Toothpicks

## Skills Learned
✔ Creative and imaginative thinking
✔ Cognitive/classification skills
✔ Fine motor skills

## What to Do

1. Go to the grocery store (or to your own refrigerator if your parents say it's okay) and pick out some veggies that you think would be good for monster parts, such as the ones listed.

2. Set them on the table and study them a few minutes, visualizing them as monster heads or facial details.

3. Get to work putting together a scary—or cute—monster using the veggies.

4. Cut up some of the veggies to use for your monster's facial details—such as his mouth, eyes, nose, ears—and for his arms and legs.

5. Break toothpicks in half.

6. Insert toothpicks into veggies to attach the facial features, arms, and legs. For example, you might use a potato as the monster's body and then attach olives for eyes, a red pepper strip for a mouth, a cherry tomato for a nose, cauliflower heads for ears, carrots for legs and arms, and alfalfa sprouts or parsley for hair.

7. Have your Veggie Monster conquer some evil Fruit Fiends.

**Safety Tips**

★ Get parental supervision when using a sharp knife.
★ Be careful with the sharp ends of the toothpicks.

# Pom-Pom Pets

Ages 7 to 12

Create your own Pom-Pom Pets to keep you company, then make them useful and put them to work.

## Materials

★ Pom-poms in a variety of colors and sizes
★ Felt scraps or squares
★ Scissors
★ Glue
★ Wiggly eyes
★ Magnetic tape

## Skills Learned

✔ Cognitive skills
✔ Fine motor development
✔ Creative and imaginative thinking

## What to Do

1. Think about what kinds of pets you want to make. You might want to create a gray mouse, a red ladybug, a green caterpillar, a yellow bumblebee, or a "purple puffalump."
2. Pick out the colors of the pom-poms you'll want to use for your pets.
3. Choose felt scraps to match, such as gray for the mouse, green for the caterpillar, and yellow for the bumblebee.
4. Cut the felt a little larger than the pom-pom to serve as the foundation for each pet. If your pet needs only one pom-pom,

such as the gray mouse, cut the gray felt into a circle a little larger than the pom-pom. If you're making the bumblebee, you might use 2 yellow pom-poms, so cut out yellow felt a little larger than both the pom-poms lined up together. If you're making the caterpillar, cut out green felt a little larger than 3 pom-poms lined up in a row.

**5.** Glue the pom-poms onto the felt foundations.

**6.** Glue on wiggly eyes and add details, such as antenna, ears, feet, and tails, cut from extra felt.

**7.** Cut a strip of magnetic tape a little smaller than the felt foundation and stick it onto the back of the felt.

**8.** Allow your Pom-Pom Pets to dry.

**9.** When your pets are ready, play with them in the following ways:

Stick them to the refrigerator to hold important messages for the family.

Set them on a cookie sheet and move them around.

Draw a road on a sheet of posterboard, put a pet on the road, and pull it along the road using a magnet underneath the posterboard.

Make them as gifts for special friends.

### More Fun

Use your imagination to create new critters from the pom-poms and felt. Give them 3 eyes, 10 legs, some wings, polka dots, sharp teeth, funny faces, and extra long bodies.

# Rainbow Scape

Ages 7 to 12

It's almost magical the way the colors appear from out of the darkness to make a beautiful, illuminated picture.

## Materials

★ Thick or firm paper, such as posterboard or cardstock paper
★ A variety of crayons
★ Black poster paint
★ Large paintbrush
★ Paper clip

## Skills Learned

✔ Cognitive skills/cause and effect
✔ Creative and imaginative thinking
✔ Fine motor development
✔ Emotional expression

## What to Do

1. Get a piece of stiff thick paper.
2. Color the paper all different colors with the crayons, filling in small sections one at a time. Press hard as you color.
3. When the paper is completely colored, cover it with a coating of black poster paint. It may take two coats of paint to completely cover the crayon.
4. While the paint is drying, think about what kind of picture you want to draw, such as a portrait, a landscape, a cartoon, or a design.

### More Fun

Draw on a sheet of white paper with crayons. Paint over the picture with black paint and see what happens.

5. Unfold a paper clip halfway so you have one end to draw with and one end to hold on to.

6. "Draw" on the black paint with the paper clip and watch the colorful image appear.

# Scrapbook

Ages 7 to 12

Scrapbooks are all the rage. But you don't need to buy an expensive kit for keeping your special memories—just make your own.

## Materials

★ Large binder
★ Construction paper or decorative paper
★ Clear Con-Tact paper
★ Hole punch
★ Scissors—with regular or scalloped edge
★ Tape or glue
★ Colored markers, puffy paints, glitter pens
★ Colored envelopes (optional)
★ Stickers, fabric scraps, ribbon, decorations
★ Mementos, collections, pictures, and so on

## Skills Learned

✔ Creative and imaginative thinking
✔ Fine motor skills
✔ Recycling materials
✔ Self-awareness and self-esteem
✔ Cognitive/organizational skills

## What to Do

1. Collect the materials you'll need to create your scrapbook.
2. Collect the objects you want to put in your scrapbook. If you want your scrapbook to have a theme, choose objects that relate to that specific theme, such as photographs of friends, trading cards, movie star pictures, vacation postcards, and so on.
3. Cover the binder with decorative paper by placing paper that's ½ inch smaller than the cover on top of the front, and glue it on. Cover with clear Con-Tact paper to preserve it.
4. Punch holes in the colored paper or decorative paper and insert it into the binder.
5. Think about how you want to organize your scrapbook— in order of sequence, events, color, size, and so on.
6. When you have your pages ready, glue or tape the objects onto the paper.
7. Cut the edges of the paper with fancy scissors if you want to make them even more decorative.
8. Using fancy pens, write titles and captions for the objects that you include in your scrapbook.
9. If you have any loose objects that can't be glued onto the paper, glue on colorful envelopes and put the objects inside.
10. Add other decorations to your scrapbook pages to make them more interesting, such as stickers, fabric scraps, ribbons, glitter, and so on.
11. Keep adding to your scrapbook as you collect more objects, and store the scrapbook in a safe place when you're not using it.

### More Fun

Make lots of scrapbooks for all kinds of collections, hobbies, and memories. Create them with your friends and share them when they're finished.

# Shoe Shiners

Ages 7 to 12

Turn your old tennis shoes into a colorful canvas and wear a work of art when you go outside.

## Materials

★ Old white tennis shoes or inexpensive new ones that your parents will let you color
★ White shoelaces
★ Colorful permanent markers, puffy paints, or fabric pens
★ Buttons, sequins, glitter
★ Embroidery floss
★ Rubber stamps
★ Scissors
★ Glue
★ Needle and thread

## Skills Learned

✔ Creative and imaginative thinking
✔ Fine motor development
✔ Recycling
✔ Self-esteem/self-expression

## What to Do

1. Set the shoes on newspaper on a table.
2. Gather a variety of materials to decorate your shoes, along with glue and scissors.
3. Use your imagination to create a whole new look for your shoes. You can sew on buttons; glue on glitter and sequins; outline rubber stamp designs with markers, paints,

or pens; sew with embroidery floss; and so on—anything to make your shoes unique and special.

4. Decorate the shoelaces with the permanent markers or fabric pens.

5. Wear your shiny new shoes outside to play.

## More Fun

Lace your shoelaces in a creative way to match your new shoes.

# 6
# Daytime Drama

Clown Kit

Costume Shop

Finger Fables

Puppet Theater

Puppet Family

Body Language

# Clown Kit

Ages 3 to 12

It's easy being a clown. Just paint your face, put on funny clothes, and act silly.

## Materials

★ 4 small bowls
★ ½ cup cornstarch
★ ¼ cup cold cream
★ Red, blue, green, and yellow food coloring
★ 4 small paintbrushes
★ Hair clips
★ Mirror
★ Oversized old colorful clothes
★ Big shoes

## Skills Learned

✔ Fine motor skills
✔ Creative and imaginative thinking
✔ Emotional expression
✔ Social interaction

## What to Do

1. Divide up the cornstarch and cold cream between the 4 bowls.
2. Tint each one with different colors of food coloring to make red, blue, green, and yellow.
3. Mix well.
4. Pin your hair back with clips and get out a mirror.

### Safety Tips

★ Be careful not to get the face paints on your good clothes and furniture.
★ Wash off your face with soap and water when you're done being a clown.

**5.** Paint your face with the different colors using the paintbrushes to look like a clown. (Try not to get the paints mixed up while you work.)

**6.** Put on funny clothes and shoes.

**7.** Act like a clown!

# Costume Shop

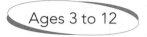

Ages 3 to 12

Create your own costume store and dress up for dramatic play so you can put on a show.

## Materials

★ *Shoes*—such as high heels, soldier boots, tap shoes, ballet slippers, sandals, cowboy boots, and fuzzy slippers

★ *Hats*—such as netted hats, military hats, cowboy hats, straw hats, beanies, and wigs

★ *Accessories*—such as costume jewelry, gloves, scarves, fur collars or wraps, belts, and socks

★ *Women's clothes*—such as nightgowns, long and short skirts, fancy dresses, and silky blouses

★ *Men's clothes*—such as vests, baggy pants, jackets, military uniforms, and suits

★ 5 cardboard boxes

## Skills Learned

✔ Creative and imaginative thinking

✔ Language and vocabulary

✔ Cognitive skills/ classification skills

✔ Social skills

✔ Self-confidence/ self-expression

## What to Do

1. Ask your parents to loan you some clothes, or go to the thrift store and buy some inexpensive clothes and accessories for your costume store. See the materials list for ideas.

2. Sort through the clothes and divide them in these 5 boxes:

   *The Shoe Department*

   *The Millinery Department* (hats and wigs)

   *The Accessory Department* (jewelry, belts, and so on)

   *Women's Wear Department*

   *Men's Wear Department*

3. Pick and choose a variety of articles of clothing and put them together in creative outfits.

4. Put on a play, using the costumes and outfits to give you ideas.

5. Change your outfits and play different roles, according to what you're wearing.

### More Fun

Get out the camera and take pictures. Then put the pictures in an album and write funny captions under each picture. Have the pictures tell a story.

# Finger Fables

Ages 3 to 12

You don't need makeup and costumes to put on a show—just your fingertips.

## Materials

★ Nontoxic fine-tip colored markers

## Skills Learned

✔ Fine motor skills
✔ Creative and imaginative thinking
✔ Emotional expression
✔ Social interaction
✔ Language and vocabulary

## What to Do

1. Get out some colored markers.
2. Think about what kind of characters you want to create for your story. You might want to make Snow White and the Seven Dwarfs (plus the Prince and the Wicked Queen), your family and friends, monsters, animals (such as 10 little monkeys), and so on.
3. Draw the characters on your fingertips with the markers.
4. If you're right-handed and have trouble drawing on your left hand (or vice versa), ask your friend to help you.
5. Put on a play with your Fingertip Friends.

## More Fun

Glue on colored string for hair, using white nontoxic glue, and make little outfits from scraps of fabric to make complete characters. You can also make finger puppets that slip on and off by cutting the fingers off plain gardening gloves and decorating them with faces, hair, and outfits.

# Puppet Theater

Ages 3 to 12

After you make the puppets, you'll need a Puppet Theater to put on a play.

## Materials

★ Scissors or sharp knife
★ Large appliance box
★ Poster paint
★ 2 pieces of scrap fabric, approximately 20 inches by 10 inches
★ Stapler or electrical tape
★ Sharp skewer
★ 2 pieces of yarn or ribbon, each 12 inches long

## Skills Learned

✔ Cognitive skills/problem solving
✔ Fine motor skills
✔ Language and vocabulary
✔ Social skills
✔ Math and measurement
✔ Creative and imaginative thinking

## What to Do

1. With your parent's supervision, cut a section of the back off the box with the scissors or knife so you can get in and out of the theater, or use the open end.
2. Cut a large rectangle in the top half of the front of the box for the puppets, about 8 by 18 inches.
3. Paint the outside of the box to make it colorful. Then paint designs or shapes on the box to make it even more fun.
4. On the inside of the box, staple or tape two pieces of fabric to cover the opening and to serve as a curtain.

**5.** Poke 2 holes in the box, 1 on each side of the curtain, and insert the ribbons. Tie back the curtain when it's show-time.

**6.** Put on a play with your puppets.

**Safety Tip**

Be careful with the scissors or knife and get a parent to supervise when you cut the box.

# Puppet Family

Ages 7 to 12

Instead of making one puppet, make a whole family that fits on one hand.

## Materials

★ 5 pom-poms in a variety of colors
★ 1 garden glove
★ Glue
★ Scissors
★ Scraps of colored felt
★ 10 wiggly eyes

## Skills Learned

✔ Creative and imaginative thinking
✔ Fine motor skills
✔ Cognitive skills/problem solving
✔ Language/vocabulary
✔ Social skills

## What to Do

**1.** Think about what kinds of puppet heads you want to make. You might want to make your family, a collection of animals, or a set of monsters.

2. Choose 5 pom-poms to be the heads of your puppets.

3. Glue the pom-poms onto the top ends of the fingers and thumb of the glove (on the palm side).

4. Glue on wiggly eyes.

5. Cut out felt bits to make mouths, ears, noses, and so on, and glue them on the pom-pom heads.

6. Now put on the glove and put on a puppet show using all your fingers and thumb, or use one finger at a time.

## More Fun

Pick out a favorite storybook, such as *Three Little Pigs*, *Peter Pan*, or *Harry Potter*, and make a puppet for each of the characters featured in the book. Then perform the story using your puppets.

# Body Language

Ages 7 to 12

You don't need words to communicate. Just use your body instead of your voice.

## Materials

★ Paper and pencil

## Skills Learned

✔ Language and communication skills
✔ Creative and imaginative thinking
✔ Body awareness
✔ Social interaction

## What to Do

1. Hand out paper and pencil to each player.
2. Have each player think of some favorite scenes from popular movies or books.
3. Take turns acting out the scenes for the others to guess using only your bodies, no words.
4. Keep score to see who guesses the most right answers.

## More Fun

Act out songs, TV shows, famous people, highlights of your life, and so on.

# 7
# Family Fun

Backyard Picnic

Adopt a Grandparent

House Detective

Chore Charts

Secret Pal

Switcharoo Sunday

# Backyard Picnic

Ages 3 to 12

Who says you have to go to the park for a picnic when you have the perfect place right in your own backyard?

## Materials

★ Blanket or plastic table-cloth
★ Paper plates, cups, plasticware, and napkins
★ Lunch or dinner
★ Picnic basket

## Skills Learned

✔ Initiative and competence
✔ Planning and carrying out plans
✔ Creative and imaginative thinking
✔ Social interaction

## What to Do

1. Ask your parents when would be a good time to have a picnic in the backyard.
2. Gather the blanket or tablecloth and picnic items listed above.
3. Plan the meal for your picnic. Try to choose foods that are easy to carry and easy to eat. For example:

   *Lunch:* Cut-up sandwiches, pita pockets, thermos of

soup, veggies and dip, fruit salad, cheese and crackers, cookies or cupcakes, thermos of lemonade or punch

*Dinner:* Barbequed chicken, hot dogs or hamburgers on the grill, potato or macaroni salad, French fries, cooked vegetables, cake or pie

4.  Prepare the food and pack it up in the picnic basket, along with the picnic items.

5.  Head for the backyard, spread the blanket or tablecloth on the ground, and enjoy your picnic.

### Safety Tips

★ Wash your hands before you handle the food and keep it refrigerated until serving or heating time.

★ If you use candles, be sure to get permission from your parents and be careful of the flame. If you use flashlights, have an extra battery on hand.

# Adopt a Grandparent

### Ages 3 to 12

If you don't have a grandparent handy, find one in your neighborhood and give him or her a special day once a week.

## Materials

★ Cookies

★ Artwork

★ Books

★ Plants

★ Photographs

★ Note paper and pen

★ Deck of cards

## Skills Learned

✔ Social skills

✔ Community service

✔ Helping others

✔ Language skills

## What to Do

1. Find a grandparent in your community by calling the local retirement center, nursing home, or senior center or by checking around the neighborhood for an older person who lives alone.

2. Ask if you can come and visit once a week during the summer.

3. Spend the week planning what you and your adopted grandparent will do on your special day. Here are some activities to think about:

   Make oatmeal cookies, chocolate brownies, or banana bread and take them over for a snack.

   Create a picture of yourself for your adopted grandparent to hang on the wall—or make one together when you get there.

   Pick out a favorite book and read it to your adopted grandparent, or have the grandparent choose a book or story.

   Bring a plant over and plant it in the yard, or set it inside the house in a sunny area.

   Get your picture taken and then bring it over in a frame you've decorated.

Bring some note paper over and write letters to friends and relatives for your grandparent if it's difficult for your grandparent to write.

Get out a deck of cards and play some card games with your adopted grandparent.

4.  Be sure to show up each week, or let your adopted grandparent know if you can't come so he or she won't be disappointed.

## Safety Tips

★ Ask your parent to help you find a grandparent to adopt and to come with you for the first visit.

★ Keep the visits short so you don't tire out your adopted grandparent.

# House Detective

Ages 3 to 12

You've lived there for some time, but how well do you and other family members know your house? Find out through a little detective work.

## Materials
★ Cassette recorder or boom box and tape
★ Polaroid camera
★ Paper and pencil

## Skills Learned
✔ Cognitive skills/ classification
✔ Problem solving and cause and effect
✔ Sensory exploration
✔ Creative and imaginative thinking

## What to Do

1. Get out the cassette recorder and insert a blank tape.
2. Make a list of sounds you hear around the house. You might include the following:

   Doorbell ringing

   Toilet flushing

   Toaster popping up

   Coffeemaker perking

   Door slamming

   Water running

   Telephone ringing

   Chair squeaking

3. Go around the house and record the sounds on your list.
4. Gather the family and play the tape.
5. Have them write down what they think each sound is.
6. Read the answers and see how well they did on their "hearing test."
7. Take turns recording sounds from inside and outside of the house to play for each other.

# More Fun

Take close-up pictures, about 2 to 3 inches away, of objects around the house using a Polaroid camera (or throwaway camera). See how many objects your family members can recognize when they see them as close-up pictures.

# Chore Charts

Ages 3 to 12

Chores don't have to be boring. They can actually be fun. Here are some entertaining ways to get through your daily duties.

## Materials
★ Large posterboard
★ Clear Con-Tact paper (or laminator at a copy store)
★ Dry-erase or washable pens
★ Stickers
★ Little prizes or snacks

## Skills Learned
✔ Responsibility
✔ Cognitive skills
✔ Problem solving and cause and effect
✔ Cooperation

## What to Do
1. Buy a large sheet of posterboard.
2. Write your name at the top of the posterboard, then, using a felt pen, draw a grid 10 columns wide by 7 rows down (more or less, depending on how many chores you have).
3. Make a list of your chores in the top row and the days of the week down the side.
4. You might include chores such as:

   Make my bed

Clean my room

Set the table

Clear my place

Feed the pets

Take out the garbage

Walk the dog

Sweep the walk

Hang up my clothes

Take a bath

### More Fun

Make a chore chart for your parents, too, and give them a special treat—such as a big kiss and hug, a handwritten poem, breakfast in bed, or new drawing—if they get all their chores done.

5. Cover the chart with clear Con-Tact paper, or have the chart laminated at the photocopy store.

6. Hang the chart on the refrigerator or bedroom door. Tie an erasable marker to string and tape it nearby so it's accessible and won't get lost.

7. Each day, check the chart and do the required chores.

8. Mark off the completed chores with the marker, or use colorful stickers to mark the finished chores.

9. At the end of each week, have your parents hide a treat near one of the chores for a special surprise. Or help your parents plan a special project or outing if all the chores are done.

# Secret Pal

Ages 7 to 12

Can you keep a secret—even from your family? It won't be easy, but it will be fun.

## Materials

★ Construction paper and pencil
★ Newspaper
★ Breakfast foods
★ Cookie dough
★ Markers

## Skills Learned

✔ Cognitive skills
✔ Making and carrying out plans
✔ Writing skills
✔ Family relationships

## What to Do

1. Choose someone in the family to be your secret pal and don't tell anyone.

2. Plan some special things to do for your pal such as:

   Write a poem or letter and hide it in your pal's drawer.

   Bring in the newspaper before your pal wakes up.

   Make breakfast and have it waiting.

   Clean up your pal's mess.

   Make a treasure hunt for your pal with a special prize at the end.

   Create and mail a card that says "Congratulations" or "You're Special."

   Do one of your pal's chores.

   Give your pal a foot massage without being seen.

   Make cookies for your pal.

   Decorate a pair of your pal's old socks with markers.

3. When the time is right, carry out your plans. Try not to get caught!

### More Fun

Be a secret pal to a grandparent, friend, or neighbor.

4. Do something every day until your pal finally catches you and the secret is out.

5. Wait a few days, then pick another person to be your secret pal.

# Switcharoo Sunday

Ages 7 to 12

Have you ever thought about what it would be like to be your parents for a little while? Find out on Switcharoo Sunday.

**Materials**
★ Parent's stuff
★ Kid's stuff

**Skills Learned**
✔ Creative and imaginative thinking
✔ Empathy
✔ Social skills
✔ Self-awareness

## What to Do

1. Ask your parents if it would be okay to choose a convenient day for you to trade places for a few hours, or even the whole day.

2. When it's time to begin, you must act like your parent while your parent acts like you. Here are some things to do:

Wear each other's clothes.

Clean each other's rooms.

Eat each other's favorite foods.

Talk like each other.

Play a game posing as each other.

Cook a meal as you act like each other.

Have a conversation about something as if you were each other.

**3.** When the time is up, talk about how it felt to be the other person. You might ask each other the following questions:

What did you like about being the other person?

What didn't you like about being the other person?

> ## More Fun
>
> Trade places with other family members or friends, or dress up like someone you admire and act the way you think they would act.

Was there anything hard about being the other person?

What would you change about being the other person?

What have you learned about what it's like to be the other person?

What do you like about being yourself?

**4.** When the game is over, enjoy being yourself again.

# 8
# Game Time

**Listen Up**

**Pudding Chase**

**Secret Shadows**

**Name Game**

**Daffy Definitions**

**Never-Ending Story**

# Listen Up

Ages 3 to 12

See how well you can make a realistic sound—and how
many sounds you can guess.

## Materials
★ Paper and pencil

## Skills Learned
✔ Listening and attention
skills
✔ Creative and imaginative
thinking
✔ Social interaction
✔ Cognitive/classification
skills

## What to Do
1. Write down the source of some familiar noises on paper,
such as "car engine," "cow," "vacuum cleaner," "airplane,"
"horn honk," "doorbell," "telephone busy signal," and so on.
2. Take turns making noises for other players and see if they
can guess what the noise comes from.
3. Have all players record a
point each time that
they guess the correct
answer.
4. Have each player count
up their points to see
how many noises they
guessed.

### More Fun
Make a noise. Have the next
player copy the first noise and
add a new noise. Continue
copying the noises in order and
adding new noises each turn until
someone forgets a noise or does
it in the wrong order.

# Pudding Chase

Ages 3 to 12

Here's a fun and tasty way to chase your friends and tag them—with a snack.

## Materials

★ Chocolate, vanilla, or butterscotch pudding mix
★ Milk
★ Plastic bowl
★ Egg beater
★ Bathing suits

## Skills Learned

✔ Gross motor development and exercise
✔ Scientific properties
✔ Math and measurement
✔ Social interaction

## What to Do

1. Mix pudding according to the package directions and allow it to set in the refrigerator.
2. When the pudding is ready, place the bowl outside on the grass.
3. Set the boundaries of the game, such as "the backyard" or "the fenced area."
4. Put on your bathing suits.
5. Choose a player to be "It."
6. That player must count to 10 while the other players run around the play area.

### More Fun

Use vanilla pudding and tint it with food coloring for added fun. Make up several bowls of different colors and see how many colors you can tag other players with before they tag you.

**7.** When whoever is "It" reaches 10, he or she must dip a finger into the pudding and then try to tag someone with the finger full of pudding.

**8.** A player is out when tagged with the pudding. Keep playing until all the players are tagged with pudding and one player is left to be "It" the next time.

**9.** Wash off the pudding with a hose between games.

# Secret Shadows

Ages 3 to 12

Can you tell what an object is if you can only see the outline? It's time to check your visual perception.

## Materials
★ Paper and pencils
★ Objects to draw

## Skills Learned
✔ Visual perception and reading skills
✔ Cognitive skills/problem solving
✔ Spatial relationships
✔ Social interaction

## What to Do
**1.** Give each player a sheet of paper and a pencil.
**2.** Send players to different rooms so they can't see each other.
**3.** Have them find something in their rooms to draw in outline form, such as a lamp, a trophy, a flower, a couch. Be

sure players *only* draw the *outline*—no details inside the outline.

4. When you have finished your drawings, gather together to see if the other players can identify the objects.

5. Repeat, going to different rooms and drawing different objects.

---

## More Fun

Take turns drawing pictures that represent song titles, popular phrases, verbs, famous people's faces, cartoon characters, movie scenes, TV shows, foods, and so on. See who can guess the drawing first.

---

# Name Game

Ages 7 to 12

Here's a challenging and exciting game to play on a lazy afternoon when it's too hot to go outside.

**Materials**
★ Paper and pencils
★ 3-minute timer, stopwatch, or watch with second hand

**Skills Learned**
✔ Cognitive/classification skills
✔ Vocabulary
✔ Social interaction

**What to Do**
1. Pass out paper and a pencil to each player.

2. Draw a grid of 1-inch boxes, 8 squares by 8 squares.

3. Across the top, write the letters of your name (first and last), up to 8 letters. For example, if your name is Becca Ward, you'd write "BECCAWAR" in the squares.

4. Brainstorm some popular categories to use for the game, such as "Fast Food Restaurants," "State Capitals," "Boys' Names," "Trees," "Candy Bars," "Jungle Animals," "School Subjects," "Rock Stars," "Storybooks," "TV Shows," and so on.

5. Down the left side, write 8 categories from your list.

6. On the word "Go!" start the timer for 3 minutes. Players must write words in each category that begin with the letter at the top. For example, if the category is "Desserts" and the first 8 letters of your name spell "BECCAWAR," you might write into the corresponding squares: "Brownie," "Éclair," "Chocolate Cake," "Caramel Corn," "Apple Pie," "W," "Applesauce," and "Raspberry Tarts."

7. If you can't think of an item in the category to match the letter, such as the "W" above, skip it and move on to the next one.

8. Fill in as many squares as you can.

9. Go back to the ones you skipped if you have time.

10. When time is up, count how many squares you filled in. Read the answers aloud to see if the squares are filled in correctly.

11. Whoever has the most squares filled in correctly wins the game.

12. Play again with different letters across the top, such as the name of your school, your street, your pet, or your state, and different categories down the side.

### More Fun

To make the game more challenging, have players cross off any answer that matches any other player's answer. Then count how many answers are left to see who wins.

# Daffy Definitions

Ages 7 to 12

How's your vocabulary? Is it as good as your imagination? If so, you'll be a winner at this game.

## Materials
★ Dictionary
★ Paper and pencils

## Skills Learned
✔ Language and vocabulary
✔ Cognitive/classification skills
✔ Social interaction
✔ Reading skills

## What to Do
1. Sit at the table with your friends and give one player the dictionary.
2. Pass out paper and a pencil to each player.

3. Have the player with the dictionary find a new word that doesn't sound familiar.

4. Announce the word to the players and have them write it down.

5. While you write down the real definition from the dictionary, the other players must make up a definition for the word. (Make the real definition sound natural so it's not obvious.)

6. Collect the papers and mix them up.

7. Read them over once to yourself so you're familiar with them. (Don't let the other players see the papers or they might recognize the handwriting.)

8. Read the definitions aloud once, then once again.

9. Have the players write down which definition they think is correct.

10. When all players have written down a guess, have them read their guesses aloud.

11. Announce the correct definition.

12. Award points to all players who guessed the right definition.

13. Award points to the player who fooled anyone with his dictionary word.

14. Award points each time a player fooled another player with his made-up definition.

15. Pass the dictionary to the next player and keep playing.

16. At the end of the game, add up the points to see who won.

## More Fun

Choose funny words from the dictionary to make the game even more fun.

# Never-Ending Story

Ages 7 to 12

It's easy to start a story with "Once upon a time," but can you keep the story going after that?

## Materials

★ Paper and pencils
★ Index cards

## Skills Learned

✔ Language and vocabulary
✔ Creative and imaginative thinking
✔ Social interaction
✔ Cognitive skills/problem solving

## What to Do

1. Divide up the index cards among the players and have each player write a word on each of their cards, such as "gross," "bulbous," "ridiculous," "pigsty," and so on.
2. Mix up the cards and stack them face down in a pile.
3. One player starts the game by picking the top card. If he doesn't know the meaning of the word, have him look it up in the dictionary.
4. That player must begin the story and

include the word written on the card, using only one sentence.

5. The next player must pick a card and continue the story, using the new word in the next sentence.

6. Keep playing until all the cards are gone.

7. Make sure the last player ends the story in a satisfying way.

## More Fun

Write down 3 words on each card and have the players use all 3 in their sentence of the never-ending story.

# 9
# Home Alone

Bedroom Makeover

Computer Fun

"All About Me" Book

Calendar Countdown

Card Shop

Miracle Makeover

Wacky Inventions

Wee World

# Bedroom Makeover

Ages 3 to 12

Spend the day giving your room a makeover, and you'll feel like you've moved to a whole new room when you're finished.

## Materials
★ Paper and pencil
★ Bags and boxes
★ Marker
★ Adhesive paper or blank stickers

## Skills Learned
✔ Planning and carrying out plans
✔ Cognitive skills/problem solving
✔ Organization and classification skills
✔ Sense of self and self-esteem

## What to Do

1. Sit in your room and jot down thoughts about how you'd like to change it. Ask yourself the following questions:

   What do I like about my room?

   What do I want to change about my room?

   How do I want to organize my things?

   How do I want to arrange my furniture?

   What do I need for my room?

   How could I make my room more fun?

2. Think about whether you want a theme for your room, such as "Soccer," "Dance," "Stuffed Animals," "Movie Stars," or "Super Heroes."

3. Draw up a list of things you need to have and what you need to do to change your room. Keep your theme in mind as you make notes.

4. Clean out your room of all the things you don't need or don't use any more. Put them in bags or boxes and donate them to charity or have a garage sale.

5. Gather things that are similar and keep them together in boxes or plastic cartons to keep them organized. Label them with stickers so they're easy to find and retrieve.

6. Rearrange your furniture for a new look. Think about where you want your bed, drawers, desk, chairs, and so on. Decide whether you want more space or lots of cubbies, nooks, and crannies for your things.

7. Think about decorations for your room to match your theme. If you have a sports-related theme, you might set out sports equipment, hang pennants from the ceiling, put up posters of athletes, and display other sports-related objects.

8. If you have any collections, such as stuffed animals, small cars, or trading cards, think about how you can display them using a clothesline and clothespins, shelf, or picture frame. Hang up bulletin boards and

## Safety Tips

★ Keep your room clean so you don't break or trip over anything.
★ Make sure you get permission from your parents if you make any major changes to your room.
★ Don't put heavy things on the walls that might fall down, and make sure your shelves aren't overloaded or wobbly.
★ Think about how you might escape your room in case there's a fire or an emergency.

dry-erase boards on which to pin mementos and write notes and announcements.

9.  Plan some special areas in your room for your projects and hobbies, such as a reading area, a table and chairs for arts and crafts, a desk for homework and writing stories, a music area for your CDs and cassettes, and so on.

10. Redo your closet so you can store your clothes and shoes easily and find them quickly. Ask your mom or dad for plastic boxes or to install shelves in the closet for storing extra stuff.

11. Add some fun stuff to your room to make it a happy place to be. You might include glow-in-the-dark stars stuck on the ceiling, a cartoon bedspread, a bunch of soft pillows, colored lights strung around the ceiling, posters of favorite places or people, or a pet bird or rat in a cage.

12. When your room is finished, spend time there enjoying it. If something doesn't work for you, change it. After all, it's your room.

# Computer Fun

Ages 3 to 12

The Internet offers a whole world of fun things to do. Just log on and check out some of the fun sites listed here.

## Materials

★ Computer (available at the library if you don't have one)

★ Internet access (available at the library)

## Skills Learned

✔ Reading and vocabulary development

✔ Writing and language

✔ Math and science skills

✔ Cognitive skills/problem solving

✔ Research and classification skills

## What to Do

1. If you're not familiar with using a computer, ask a family member or friend to help you. Once you're online, you'll only need to know how to type in the Web addresses to get the information.

2. Use a search engine such as Yahoo, Google, or AskJeeves for general information. Type in the key word you're looking for, such as "dinosaurs," "Snoopy," "Harry Potter," or "*NSYNC," and check out the sites that come up.

### Safety Tips

★ Follow your parent's rules for using the Internet so you don't get into trouble by running up large bills, running into bad people, or going to sites that are not appropriate for kids.

★ Never give your full name, age, phone number, e-mail address, home address, or other personal information to anyone on the Internet. And never agree to meet with someone you've met on the Internet.

★ Special Note to Parents: Consider using Cyber Angels for Internet filtering software (http://cyberangels.org).

**3.** Here are some great sites you might want to explore:

http://www.kidnews.com—Read news from kids all over the nation and contribute your own news.

http://www.ks-connection.org—Find a pen pal to write to and make a new friend.

http://www.cyberkids.com—Check out "Fun and Games" for puzzles, stories, and games.

http://www.exploratorium.edu—Visit this interactive science lab for experiments and information.

http://www.funbrain.com/math —Have fun playing games with math.

http://www.solarviews.com/eng/homepage.htm—Find out more about our solar system.

http://www.encyclopedia.com—Look up anything you want to know about.

http://kids.mysterynet.com—Read and solve short mysteries and write your own mystery stories.

http://www.kidsdomain.com/games/index.html—Find games, activities, and all kinds of fun.

http://www.bluemountain.com—Make greeting cards for your friends and family.

http://www.magickeys.com/books/index.html—Read stories online, complete with pictures and sound effects.

http://www.funology.com—Find all kinds of fun to keep you from being bored.

http://www.conjuror.com/magictricks—Learn how to do magic tricks and amaze your friends!

**4.** Learn to create your own Web page. For help, go to http://www.lissaexplains.com/intro.shtml or http://www.ipl.org/youth/kidsweb.

# "All About Me" Book

Ages 7 to 12

You're about to write the most interesting book on the planet—it's all about you. And what could be more fascinating?

**Materials**

★ Blank journal, scrapbook, or pad of construction paper

★ Pen and colored markers, glitter pens, glow pens, or iridescent pens

★ Tape, scissors, glue

★ Pictures of yourself

★ Mementos from your life

**Skills Learned**

✔ Writing and language skills

✔ Cognitive skills

✔ Creative and imaginative thinking

✔ Self-esteem and self-awareness

**What to Do**

**1.** Buy a blank book or scrapbook, or make your own book by putting together several sheets of construction paper, punching holes along one side, and tying the book together with yarn or ribbon.

2. Think about your life and spend a few minutes jotting down some of the highlights that you can remember. You might include such things as your birthday parties over the years, your first days at school, your first friend, your family vacations, your achievements, and your special memories.

3. Arrange them in order and see if you can find pictures or mementos to go with them.

4. When you've got your memories and mementos ready, begin your "All About Me" book.

5. On the cover, put your baby picture and a picture of yourself today. Decorate the cover with designs using fancy pens.

6. On the first page, write down your birth statistics. You can ask your parents for the information or find it in your baby book. Include the following: Birth weight, height, time and date of birth, birthplace, birth order (first born, for example), who your parents are, any siblings you have, and anything else related to your birth. Include a picture if you like, or draw a picture of yourself as a baby.

7. On the next page, include memories of your babyhood (or things your parents told you), such as your first birthday, your first tooth, your first step, your first food, and so on.

8. Continue adding pages for each year of your life, and include pictures, mementos, and drawings to represent those special moments. Add information about your friends, pets, special days, special achievements, birthdays, vacations, toys, dolls, TV shows, music, and everything else you can think of about yourself.

9. You might also include your dreams, thoughts about the future, and ideas you have planned for yourself.

10. Decorate each page with stickers, designs using your fancy pens, and funny comments about your pictures and mementos.

11. After you've reached your current age, add enough pages to take you to age 18 so you can continue your book.

## Safety Tips

★ Get permission to use pictures from your past so your parents won't get mad that you messed up the family album.

★ Be careful with the scissors, glue, and pens.

12. Tuck the book away in a safe place and keep collecting memories and mementos to put in your "All About Me" book. Get it out now and then and add to it.

13. Check the library or Internet for news events that happened during each year of your life and add them to your book, such as who was president, what movies were playing, and important events that took place at that time. Make a Family Tree to go with your Me Book by asking your parents about your relatives and ancestors.

14. When you reach 18, you'll have a complete book all about you.

# Calendar Countdown

Ages 7 to 12

Fill the days with fun things to do and make your summer the best it can be.

## Materials

★ 3 large sheets of paper or posterboard
★ Calendar
★ Colored markers
★ A copy of *Summer Smarts for Cool Kids*
★ Paper and pencil

## Skills Learned

✔ Cognitive skills/brainstorming
✔ Planning and carrying out plans
✔ Creative and imaginative thinking
✔ Fine motor skills
✔ Competence and self-confidence

## What to Do

1. Draw a grid on the large sheets of paper, using the calendar pages for June, July, and August as an example.
2. Label the days of the weeks along the top.
3. Number the days of each month according to the calendar example.
4. Use the *Summer Smarts for Cool Kids* book as a guide for ideas. Read it over and choose the ones you like the most.
5. Write down the ideas on a sheet of paper, along with the page numbers.
6. Brainstorm some more ideas for things to do during the summer, such as "Go to the library," "Play soccer," "Take an art class," and so on.

7. Spread the calendar pages out so you can see what your summer looks like.

8. Circle your family vacation days on the calendar.

9. Fill in any other important days coming up during the summer.

10. Fill in each day with an idea for something to do so that every day offers an activity and looks fun. Name each day to make it even more special, such as "Miracle Makeover Day," "Colossal Cookie Day," and so on.

11. Follow the suggestions each day during the summer, unless something else comes up. Then just postpone the activity to another day.

**Safety Tip**

If you have an activity planned but the weather or other circumstances don't permit it, be flexible. Trade around some activities so you still have something to do and don't get bored.

# Card Shop

Ages 7 to 12

Have you ever forgotten a birthday or another special occasion? Set up your own greeting card company and be ready for all those special days ahead.

## Materials

★ Construction paper or decorative paper
★ Colored markers, glitter pens, or puffy pens
★ Rubber stamps, stickers, decals
★ Calendar or *Chase's Annual Events* (a book you can find at the library)
★ List of special occasions for your friends and relatives
★ Envelopes
★ Stickers (optional)

## Skills Learned

✔ Writing and communication skills
✔ Reading skills
✔ Creative and imaginative thinking
✔ Social relationships

## What to Do

1. Find some colorful or decorative paper you can use for making cards.
2. Fold the paper in half, then in half again to make the card.
3. Choose a special friend or relative and a special occasion for your card.
4. Plan what you want to say on the front and inside of the card. You might make up a poem, write something humorous, or personalize it with a short anecdote or memory.
5. Write your message using fancy letters and fancy pens. Leave room for some illustrations.
6. Add appropriate drawings to match the message. You can draw your own or use cartoons, rubber stamps, stickers, or decals to illustrate your card.

7.  Put your card in an envelope, write the correct address on the outside, stick a stamp on it, and mail it to your special friend or relative.

8.  Make some more cards and have them ready for special occasions that are coming up.

## More Fun

If you have a computer, you might want to make your cards using a card template, or create your own. There are card packages you can buy to help you make your cards on the computer. If you don't know any special occasions coming up, go to the library and find a book called *Chase's Annual Events*. You'll discover lots of reasons to celebrate every day of the year, such as "Mickey Mouse's Birthday," "Summer Solstice," and even "National Nothing Day."

# Miracle Makeover

Ages 7 to 12

Tired of looking the same every day? Now is your chance to create a whole new you—with a Miracle Makeover. Don't worry—it's only temporary.

## Materials

★ Mirror

★ Old shirt

★ Makeup items—such as blush, powder, eye liner, and lipstick—or face paints to make a monster or clown face

★ Hairbrush and comb

★ Hair accessories, such as scrunchies, rubber bands, clips, ribbons, and so on

★ Hair spray, gels, and temporary spray hair color

★ Wigs, hats, hairpieces, scarves, glasses, foil (for braces), eye liner (for freckles), and so on

★ Camera

## Skills Learned

✔ Cognitive skills/cause and effect

✔ Creative and imaginative thinking

✔ Fine motor skills

✔ Self-awareness and self-esteem

## What to Do

1. Get out a mirror and put on a large old shirt or smock.

2. Gather all kinds of makeover items, such as the ones listed above, and set them on a table next to the mirror.

3. Experiment with the makeup or face paints to create a whole new look for yourself. You might use the makeup to transform yourself into a movie star, a monster, an old person, a cartoon character, or an animal.

4. Do your hair to fit your new face with the brush, comb, and hair accessories. You might try backcombing your

hair (holding the ends and combing toward the scalp rather than the regular way from scalp to ends) to make it stick out; use gels to spike and shape it; or color it blue, green, or rainbow with temporary spray hair colors.

5.  Add a wig, hat, scarf, glasses, foil braces, freckles, and other items to enhance your new look.

6.  Enjoy your new face and be sure to take pictures of yourself—to surprise your friends and family.

### Safety Tips

★ Get your parents' permission if you're using their makeup or hair products.
★ Be careful when using makeup and hair products around your eyes.
★ Check to make sure the makeup will come off. You don't want to go out in public like that, do you?

# Wacky Inventions

Ages 7 to 12

It's amazing what you can come up with when you use your imagination—just like all those famous inventors.

## Materials

★ A variety of objects for your invention, such as small boxes, containers, pipe cleaners, wire, string, yarn, Popsicle sticks, wood scraps, empty bottles and cans, paper, foil, cardboard, fabric scraps, rubber bands, toothpicks, and so on

★ Tape, scissors, glue, stapler, dull knife

★ Colored markers

★ Paper and pencil

## Skills Learned

✔ Creative and imaginative thinking

✔ Problem solving/cause and effect

✔ Understanding scientific properties

✔ Math and measurement

✔ Cognitive skills

✔ Planning and carrying out plans

## What to Do

1. Collect as many objects as you can to use for your wacky invention.

2. Set them on the table along with some craft tools listed above.

3. Think about what you'd like to invent, such as a pet washer, a clothes sorter, a door closer, a book holder, or anything you've been wishing you had to make life easier.

4. Draw a picture of your invention on paper.

5. Think about what objects you'll need to make your invention and label them on the diagram.

6. Now put your invention together, following your diagram.

7. See how it turns out. If problems arise while you're working, try to figure out a way to solve them.

8. When your invention is finished, try it out and see if it works.

9. Write down the instructions so others can make your invention, too.

10. If it's really great, consider getting a United States patent (which means you'll be the only one who can make your product!)

**More Fun**

Make a contraption that sends a marble through a complicated course from start to finish.

# Wee World

Ages 7 to 12

Honey, you shrunk the world! Make your own mini-city, tiny house, little lost world, or whatever world you like.

## Materials

★ Shoebox or other small box
★ Colored construction paper
★ Scissors, tape, glue
★ Markers
★ Miniature people or animals
★ Miniature objects and accessories, such as furniture, trees, buildings, and so on

## Skills Learned

✔ Creative and imaginative thinking
✔ Cognitive skills/problem solving
✔ Planning and carrying out plans
✔ Spatial relationships
✔ Fine motor skills

## What to Do

1. Find a small box in which to build your wee world.

2. Remove the top and turn the box on its side.

3. Think about what you want to make and how you plan to go about it. You might consider the following: a dinosaur world, a city or your own town, a hospital, a school, a mall, a space station, a courtroom, a police station, a doll house, or a scene from a favorite book, such as a Harry Potter or Dr. Seuss story.

4. Cut out construction paper to make the walls, ceiling, and floor. Use appropriate colors to match your world, such as green for dinosaur world, blue sky and white streets for the city, or a variety of colors for your dollhouse. Glue the paper onto the inside of the box.

5. Think about the things you want to have in your city. If you're making a dinosaur world, you'll want trees, a volcano, and a lake. If you're making a city, you'll want to include tall buildings, a park, and streets. Buy the objects at a hobby store or make them yourself by cutting, folding, and taping construction paper into the appropriate shapes.

6. Add details to the objects using colored markers.

7. Use miniature figures you already have or buy some little people or animals to set into your tiny world or to play with, using your world as a background. For example, if you're making a dinosaur world, you'll need tiny dinosaurs. If it's a city, include tiny people.

8. Imagine life in your wee world and use the little figures to tell a story.

### More Fun

Make individual city buildings, such as a post office, school, hospital, library, restaurant, grocery store, and so on, using another box for each. Then set them all up to make a whole city.

# 10
# Kids in the Kitchen

Silly Smiles

Hamburger Cookies

Cookie-on-a-Stick

Cheesy Quesadilla

Colossal Cookie

Dirt and Worms Dessert

Kitty Litter Cake

Shark Attack!

# Silly Smiles

Ages 3 to 12

If you're having a bad day (or even if you aren't!), here's a way to put a silly smile on your face—and in your mouth.

## Materials

★ 1 red apple
★ Sharp knife and dull knife
★ Plate
★ ½ cup peanut butter, cream cheese, or spread-able cheese
★ 16 tiny cubes of cheese, about the size of big teeth
★ 4 dried apricots (optional)
★ ¼ cup grated cheese (optional)
★ 8 to 10 raisins (optional)

## Skills Learned

✔ Reading and following directions
✔ Creative and imaginative thinking
✔ Good nutrition
✔ Math and measurement

## What to Do

1. Slice the apple into 8 pieces, by first slicing it in half, then slicing each half in half, then slice those quarters in half. You should have 8 slices, which will form the lips of your silly smiles.

2. Spread the peanut butter or cheese spread (for gums) on one side of an apple wedge.

3. Place 4 cheese cubes on top of the wedge to form teeth.

4. Spread the peanut butter or cheese spread on another apple wedge and place it on top of the cheese cubes to form a big silly smile.

5. Repeat for remaining wedges to make a total of 4 smiles.

6. Eat the silly smiles with your own silly smile.

### More Fun

Add a dried apricot for a tongue in between the teeth, and sprinkle some grated cheese on top for a mustache. Use a few raisins instead of the cheese cubes to make some bad teeth, or use colored mini-marshmallows for funny teeth.

# Hamburger Cookies

Ages 3 to 12

They look just like miniature hamburgers—but they taste like crunchy cookies.

## Materials

★ 20 vanilla wafers

★ Large plate

★ 10 chocolate cookies such as Snackwells, chocolate-covered Oreos, chocolate-covered mint sandwiches

★ Red, yellow, and green tubes of frosting

★ Small tube of yellow gel icing

★ Sesame seeds

## Skills Learned

✔ Reading and following directions

✔ Math and measurement

✔ Creative and imaginative thinking

## What to Do

1. Place 2 vanilla wafers on a plate, flat sides up, to make the hamburger bun.

2. On 1 cookie, squeeze a dot of red frosting on ⅓ of the cookie (for catsup), a dot of yellow frosting on ⅓ of the cookie (for mustard), and a dot of green frosting on ⅓ of cookie (for lettuce.)

3. Repeat for the other vanilla wafer.

4. Place a chocolate cookie on top of one of the frosted vanilla wafers and top it with the other vanilla wafer so the chocolate cookie is in between the frosted sides of the vanilla wafers.

5. Press the cookies together to secure them. This causes the frosting to seep out on the sides a little so it looks even more like a hamburger.

6. Place a small dot of yellow gel icing in the center of the top cookie and spread it around with a clean finger.

7. Use your other hand to sprinkle on a few sesame seeds (so the seeds won't stick to your fingers) to make it look like a sesame seed bun.

8. Enjoy your Hamburger Cookie. You want fries with that?

---

### More Fun

See if you can make up some other treats that look like real foods to fool your friends, such as pizza cookies (large round cookies covered with red icing and decorated with coconut, tiny sprinkles, and candies to look like toppings).

---

# Cookie-on-a-Stick

Ages 3 to 12

Turn plain old cookies into funny-faced puppets you can eat right off the stick.

## Materials

★ Refrigerator sugar cookie dough or your own favorite sugar cookie recipe
★ Flour
★ Rolling pin
★ Glass or bowl to use as cookie cutter
★ Popsicle sticks or tongue depressors
★ Cookie sheet
★ Tubes of colored icing
★ Decorative sprinkles and candies

## Skills Learned

✔ Reading and following directions
✔ Creative and imaginative thinking
✔ Social interaction

## What to Do

1. Make your favorite sugar cookie recipe, or use store-bought refrigerator sugar cookie dough.

2. Sprinkle flour on a board and roll out the dough to about ¼-inch thick, occasionally sprinkling flour on top of the dough so it doesn't stick to the rolling pin.

3. Preheat the oven according to package or recipe directions. (Get your parent's permission to use the oven.)

4. Cut out circles from the dough using glasses or bowls, depending on how big you want your cookie heads.

5. Transfer the circles to the cookie sheet, setting them about an inch apart.

6. Carefully insert Popsicle sticks into each cookie.

7. Bake according to package or recipe directions.

8. Allow to cool.

9. Use tube of frosting to decorate the cookie, and add decorative sprinkles and candies to make funny faces.

10. Put on a Cookie Puppet Show with your friends, then eat your Cookies-on-a-Stick.

# More Fun

Use some animal cookie cutters instead of circles to make a variety of Animals-on-a-Stick. Create your own shapes using dull knives to cut out the cookies. Make copies of your friends' and family members' faces on the cookies, then present them to the models.

# Cheesy Quesadilla

Ages 7 to 12

Kids love quesadillas, the Mexican finger food. They're easy to make, easy to eat, and easy to clean up.

## Materials

★ 1 corn or flour tortilla
★ Microwave plate
★ ¼ cup shredded cheddar or Monterey jack cheese
★ Sour cream and salsa (optional)
★ *Additional options:* chopped olives, chopped tomatoes, bacon bits or pieces of ham, guacamole
★ Knife

## Skills Learned

✔ Following instructions
✔ Fine motor development
✔ Math and measuring
✔ Scientific properties
✔ Cognitive skills/cause and effect

## What to Do

1. Put the tortilla on a microwave plate.
2. Sprinkle cheese over the tortilla.
3. Microwave the tortilla for 30 to 40 seconds on high, until cheese is melted. Heat another 5 to 10 seconds if the cheese isn't melted.

### Safety Tip

Be careful when removing the hot plate from the microwave so you don't burn yourself.

**4.** Carefully remove the plate from microwave.

**5.** Fold the quesadilla in half and press it together.

**6.** Cut into triangles with a knife.

**7.** Spread on sour cream and dip into salsa, if you like.

# Colossal Cookie

Ages 7 to 12

You won't be able to fit this cookie in your mouth all at once, so plan to share it with your family and friends.

## Materials

★ Favorite cookie recipe, such as chocolate chip, oatmeal raisin, or peanut butter, or refrigerator cookie dough

★ Cookie sheet

★ Vegetable spray

★ Toothpick

★ Large sheet of cardboard

★ Foil

★ Tubes of frosting in a variety of colors and decorator tips

★ Decorative edible sprinkles

## Skills Learned

✔ Reading and following directions

✔ Math and measurement skills

✔ Understanding scientific properties

✔ Creative and imaginative thinking

## What to Do

1. Prepare cookie dough according to package directions, or unwrap refrigerator dough.
2. Cover cookie sheet with foil, then spray foil with vegetable spray.
3. Press cookie dough onto sheet and shape it into a large circle, heart, or other shape, about ½-inch thick.
4. Bake according to package directions, but add a few extra minutes to make sure it's done in the middle and lightly browned on top. Check by inserting a toothpick. If it comes out clean, the cookie is done. Watch that the cookie doesn't burn.
5. Cut out a piece of cardboard the same shape as the cookie but a little larger.
6. Cover the cardboard with foil.
7. Allow the cookie to cool, then loosen the bottom with a spatula and slide it onto the foil-covered cardboard.
8. Decorate the cookie with frosting tubes and sprinkles, any way you like. You might write a special message in the middle, such as "Happy Birthday Dad" or "Celebrate Summer Solstice" (a time of year when the sun is farthest from the celestial equator). Then wrap it in plastic wrap to keep it fresh. Show off your Colossal Cookie, then break it into pieces and share with friends and family.

## Safety Tips

★ Get a parent to supervise while using the oven, and be careful not to burn yourself while handling the hot cookie sheet and cookie.
★ Don't try to eat that whole cookie by yourself—you'll get a tummy ache. Besides, it's more fun to share!

**9.** You could also use a specially shaped cake pan for baking your cookie, such as a cartoon character or animal, and then decorate it to fit the shape. Invite your friends to help you.

# Dirt and Worms Dessert

Ages 7 to 12

Surprise your friends with this special dessert that looks like it came directly from the backyard.

## Materials

★ 1-quart size flower pot
★ Foil
★ 1 package chocolate pudding mix or 4 to 6 pudding cups
★ 1 package chocolate wafer cookies
★ Plastic bag
★ Rolling pin
★ 8 to 12 gummy worms
★ Fake flower or plant
★ Trowel
★ Small bowls and spoons

## Skills Learned

✔ Following instructions
✔ Fine motor development
✔ Math and measurement
✔ Scientific properties
✔ Creative and imaginative thinking

## What to Do

1. Line the flower pot with foil.
2. Mix chocolate pudding according to package directions.
3. Fill the flower pot with the pudding mix, or scoop out pudding cups into pot.
4. Place chocolate wafer cookies into a plastic bag and crush them with a rolling pin until they look like dirt.
5. Scoop the cookie crumbs on top of pudding.
6. Stick gummy worms into the "dirt."
7. Insert a fake flower or plant in the middle of the pot.
8. Set the pot on the table as a centerpiece and scoop the "dirt" into small bowls with the clean trowel.

## Safety Tips

★ Be careful you don't squish your fingers while crushing the cookies.
★ Make sure the plastic bag doesn't tear, or you'll have crumbs everywhere. You may want to double-bag the cookies before you crush them.

# Kitty Litter Cake

Ages 7 to 12

If you really want to gross out your family and friends, make this hilarious dessert and watch them laugh up a fur ball.

## Materials

★ Spice or other favorite cake mix
★ Large foil cake pan
★ New plastic kitty litter pan
★ Large spoon
★ Can of white frosting
★ Dull knife
★ Package of peanut butter, spice, or oatmeal sandwich cookies
★ Plastic bag
★ Rolling pin
★ Green food coloring
★ 4 to 5 large Tootsie Rolls
★ Microwave plate
★ New kitty litter scoop

## Skills Learned

✔ Reading and following instructions
✔ Understanding scientific properties
✔ Math and measurement
✔ Sense of humor

## What to Do

1. Prepare cake mix according to package directions and bake in foil pan until done.

2. Set the foil pan with the cake inside the new kitty litter pan.

3. Cover the top of the cake with frosting.

4. Put the cookies in a plastic bag and crush them with a rolling pin.

5. Set about ⅓ of the crushed cookies aside.

6. Sprinkle the remaining cookie crumbs over the cake.

7. Tint the set-aside crumbs with several drops of green food coloring and mix well (to make them look like the chlorophyll in kitty litter).

8. Sprinkle green crumbs over top of cake.

9. Place Tootsie Rolls on microwave plate and heat in microwave for about 15 seconds. Check to see if the rolls have begun to soften, but be careful not to melt them.

10. When the Tootsie Rolls are soft, taper the ends into points.

11. Place the Tootsie Rolls on top of the cake. (Guess what they're supposed to be!)

12. Set the cake on newspapers on the table and serve it with the new kitty litter scoop.

**Safety Tip**

Ask your parents to supervise when you're using the oven. And watch out for the fur balls your guests will cough up when they see this cake!

# Shark Attack!

Ages 7 to 12

Don't worry—these sharks won't bite you. You get to bite them first. Then gobble them up.

## Materials

★ 1 package green gelatin (sugar-free preferred)
★ 1 package blue gelatin (sugar-free preferred)
★ 1 cup boiling water
★ 1 cup cold water
★ 20 to 25 gummy sharks
★ 1 cup lowfat, low-sugar whipped topping
★ Blue food coloring (optional)
★ Large clean fishbowl or clear plastic or glass bowl

## Skills Learned

✔ Reading and following directions
✔ Math and measurement
✔ Understanding scientific properties
✔ Creative and imaginative thinking

## What to Do

1. Make green gelatin according to package directions.
2. Place a few gummy sharks into the bottom of the bowl.
3. Pour gelatin into fish bowl or clear bowl and place in refrigerator to set, about 2 to 3 hours, until jiggly.
4. Make blue gelatin according to package directions.

5. Place a few more gummy sharks on top of the firm green gelatin.

6. Pour blue gelatin on top and place it in the refrigerator to set, another 2 to 3 hours.

7. When firm, spread on a layer of whipped topping to make waves. Tint the topping with a little blue food coloring if you like.

8. Stick a few gummy sharks in the topping and serve in individual dishes.

# More Fun

Think up other ways to use gelatin to create fun foods, such as these:
★ "Bugs in Amber" (gummy bugs in yellow gelatin)
★ "Hot Lava" (candy rocks in red gelatin)
★ "Rainbow" (layer 6 colors of gelatin to make a rainbow)

# 11
# Moneymakers

Car Wash

Everything Goes! Yard Sale

Neighborhood News

Roadside Café

Pampered Pet Services

# Car Wash

Ages 7 to 12

Make money and keep cool at the same time with a do-it-yourself car-wash business.

## Materials

★ Large bucket or pan
★ Car-wash soap or dish-washing liquid
★ Large sponge
★ Hose and nozzle
★ Water
★ Several old towels

## Skills Learned

✔ Cognitive skills/problem solving
✔ Fine and gross motor skills/exercise
✔ Money management
✔ Planning and carrying out plans

## What to Do

1. Ask around the neighborhood to see if anyone needs a car wash, or make signs and hang them up to drum up some business.
2. When it's time to do a car wash, here's what to do:
3. Pour a few tablespoons of car-wash soap or dish soap into a large bucket.
4. Fill the bucket with water.
5. Attach a nozzle to the hose and spray the car all over to get rid of the loose dirt.
6. Soak a large sponge in the water.

**7.** Use the wet sponge to wash the car. Hold it firmly, but don't scrub so hard that you scratch the paint.

**8.** Wash everything from top to bottom, including the hub-caps, the bumpers, the mirrors, the windows, and the top (you may need to stand on a small stool if you can't reach the top).

**9.** Rinse off the soap with the hose. Make sure you get all the soap off.

**10.** Dry the car with the towels. The car really gets clean with this step, so do a good job with the towel.

**11.** If you have a mini-vacuum, you might vacuum the inside of the car, too—for an extra fee, of course.

**12.** Have the car owner look over your work, then collect your money, thank him for the business, and find another car to wash.

**13.** Have a friend help you. That way you can split the work as well as the money.

### Safety Tip

Don't use anything besides a sponge on the car so you don't ruin the paint.

# Everything Goes! Yard Sale

Ages 7 to 12

Here's a fun way to make some extra cash—and get rid of all those things you don't use any more. Just don't sell the yard!

## Materials

★ Plain stickers

★ Markers

★ Posterboard

★ Cashbox

★ Money

★ Table and chair

★ Calculator

★ Paper and pencil

## Skills Learned

✔ Math skills

✔ Money management

✔ Cognitive skills

✔ Social skills

## What to Do

1. Go through your toys, games, clothes, and other objects and choose the ones that you don't use or like or have outgrown. Check with your parents to make sure they approve of the objects you have chosen to sell.

2. Think about what each item is worth. Here are some questions to consider:

   How new or old is it?

   What condition is it in?

   What did it cost originally?

   What do you think it's worth now?

   What would you pay for it now?

   Will you take less if you're offered less for it?

3. Put stickers on all the objects and write the price. If several people are participating in the yard sale, put your initials on the stickers, too.

4. Use the posterboard to make posters for the sale. For each poster, be sure to:

   Include the day and time of the sale (weekends are best).

Put the address of the sale (and maybe an arrow pointing the way).

List some of the objects you're selling (if you have room on the poster).

Write the words large and thick so they're easy to read from a distance.

Tape or tack the posters to poles in your neighborhood (and remove them after the sale!).

**5.** Get a good night's sleep. You'll have to get up early to set up for the sale. And buyers like to get an early start.

**6.** In the morning, arrange the items in the front yard or driveway so they are easy to see and handle.

**7.** Set up your cashbox at a small table, ready for use. *Always* keep an eye on your cashbox. Never leave it unattended.

**8.** Place the calculator, paper, and pencil on the table, too.

**9.** Greet the buyers as they arrive and ask if they have any questions, then let them browse.

**10.** If someone offers you less than the sticker price, consider bargaining with them by asking for a little more than the offer.

**11.** When you make the sale, remove the stickers and place them on the paper. If you agree to sell an

## Safety Tips

★ Always watch your cashbox and other important or expensive items so the buyers don't accidentally walk off with them.

★ Have a friend or relative help you with the sale so one can watch the cash and the other can help the customers.

★ Make sure a parent is on the premises during the sale in case you need help.

★ Don't sell your father's favorite golf clubs—or anything else someone in your family values!

item for less, change that sticker price to match the actual sale price. Add up the amounts using the calculator or your math skills and tell the buyer the total.

12. Complete the sale by making change from the money in your cashbox. Double-check your math to make sure you give back the correct amount.

13. Count up your money at the end of the day and divide up the amounts according to the initials on the stickers.

14. Consider giving the remaining unsold items to a thrift shop or other charity.

# Neighborhood News

Ages 7 to 12

Grab your notebook and scour the streets for the latest news to publish in your own *Neighborhood News* (or name it whatever you like). You may be surprised what you find out.

## Materials
★ Newspaper
★ Index cards
★ Black marker
★ Reporter's notebook and pencil
★ Computer
★ Computer paper

## Skills Learned
✔ Creative writing and language development
✔ Planning and organization
✔ Math and money skills
✔ Social interaction
✔ Community awareness
✔ Managing a small business

## What to Do

1. Get out your local newspaper and look it over to see how a newspaper is put together.

2. Write down the sections you want to include in your newspaper, such as the front page headlines, "People" section, comics page, want-ads, "Entertainment" section, and "Vital Statistics."

3. Take your notebook and pencil and stop by each neighbor to see what their latest news is. (Be sure you know the people you're interviewing and stay in your own neighborhood so you'll be safe.) You might ask them the following questions to get them started talking:

   What's new in your family?—*Headline News*

   What's up with the kids?—*People Section*

   What are you doing this weekend—*Entertainment Section*

   Do you have anything you want to sell, do you have any odd jobs available, or have you lost anything? —*Want-Ads*

   Has anything funny happened lately?—*Comics*

   Has anyone gotten engaged, married, given birth, moved, or died?—*Vital Statistics*

4. After you've jotted down all the news in your notebook, head for the computer to type it in.

5. First design your newspaper pages so you know where everything goes.

6. Type in the most interesting news you have learned for each section. Make sure you include all the basic details in news reporting: who, what, when, where, why, and how. Start with the most interesting part of the news to grab your reader's attention and then fill in the details.

**7.** Add headlines (titles) to each of your stories to interest your readers. Use a large, fancy font for the headlines to make the paper more interesting to read.

**8.** Leave sections of the paper blank so you can add photos, drawings, or cartoons.

**9.** Print out the news on computer paper.

**10.** Fill in the blank areas by taping on photos, cartoons, and so on. If you have a digital camera or scanner, you might take photos and place them in the text that way.

**11.** Count how many copies of the newspaper you want to publish and take it to an inexpensive copy store to reproduce it, or use your own printer if you don't need too many copies.

**12.** Keep track of your costs and then decide how much to charge for your newspaper so you make a small profit for your time and work.

**13.** Go around to the neighbors and ask if they'd like to buy a copy of your newspaper. Be sure to tell neighbors when they are mentioned in your paper. You might even hint about all the great news inside your paper to encourage them to buy one.

## More Fun

Add a new section to your newspaper each edition, such as "Sports"—what the local kids are playing, "Business"—where people are working and how their jobs are going, "Community News"—what's happening in town, "Food"—a favorite recipe from a neighbor, and "Dear Nabby"—an advice column written by a secret columnist (you!).

**14.** When you're finished selling the papers, add up how much money you made selling your papers, then subtract your cost total to see if you made a profit.

**15.** Begin planning your next edition of the *Neighborhood News*.

# Roadside Café

Ages 7 to 12

The secret to a successful business is location, product, and service. If you offer all three, your Roadside Café should be a hit.

## Materials
★ 2 to 3 large posterboards
★ Colored markers
★ Tape
★ Card table or other small table
★ Chairs
★ Drinks, such as lemonade, apple juice, orange juice, grape juice, water
★ Snacks, such as cookies, cupcakes, brownies, crispy treats
★ Containers and plates to hold drinks and treats
★ Money holder and change

## Skills Learned
✔ Responsibility and business management
✔ Cognitive skills/problem solving
✔ Math and money skills
✔ Creative and imaginative thinking
✔ Social skills

## What to Do

1. Think about the three elements of having a successful business—location, product, and service.

   *Location*—Where would be the best place for your café? On the driveway or the sideway, or in the front yard? (Be sure to get permission before you start.)

   *Product*—What do you want to sell? Drinks? Snacks? Other items?

   *Service*—How to you want to handle your business? Sell the products yourself? Hire someone to help out? Be friendly or be businesslike? Keep good hours and offer a good product?

2. Once you've decided what, where, and how you want to sell, design 2 to 3 posters to advertise your business, using the colored markers. Make the letters large and easy to read, add some cartoon illustrations or magazine pictures of the product, and include some phrases that help attract customers and sell the product, such as "Yummy!" "Refreshing!" "Ice Cold!" "Cures Bad Breath!"

3. Prepare your product. Instead of just offering lemonade, think about offering a variety of choices, such as the drinks listed. Add cookies, cupcakes, and brownies so the customers have something to eat as well as drink—and you therefore have opportunity to make more money. Be sure your product is safe to eat and that you've made all your products with clean hands and utensils and handled them carefully. You don't want to poison your customers!

4. Think about how much you want to charge for your product. First figure out how much it will cost you to make the product and then figure out how much money you want to make over the cost. Also think about how

much people will pay for your product. If you set a high price for your product, you may not sell much; but if your price is too low, you may sell a lot but not make much money.

5. Set up your table and chairs in a convenient location that's easy for customers to access.

6. Hang one sign on the front of the table, using tape to hold it up. Hang the other two signs on poles or trees a few feet from the table on either side, to attract customers. Add arrows if you like, to help them find the café. Set out your products. Keep everything cold by using a lot of ice and storing the drinks and foods in coolers, away from the sun and heat.

7. If you have trouble attracting customers, you might pass out flyers, wave to passersby, wear funny costumes for attention, or get some kids to come to your café and act like enthusiastic customers.

8. Always be pleasant to your customers and ask them if they want something extra with their purchase, such as a brownie or drink. You might bargain with them and offer 3 items for the price of 2, if this will encourage customers to buy and still give you a profit.

9. At the end of the day, count up your money, see what your profit is (subtract your costs from your sales), and figure out if you earned enough to make your effort

## Safety Tips

★ Be cautious with strangers. Don't go anywhere with them, don't talk to them without someone else present, and make sure an adult is nearby if you need help.

★ Stay in plain sight and operate your business with a friend, for safety.

worth your time. Give the leftovers to friends, family, or a nearby retirement or homeless center.

# Pampered Pet Services

Ages 7 to 12

If you love animals, this is the job for you. Offer the neighborhood pets your pet-sitting, pet-walking, and pet-washing services for cash.

## Materials

### Pet-Sitting and Pet-Walking

★ Book on animal care
★ Construction paper
★ Colorful markers
★ Large posterboard for signs
★ Piggy bank

### Pet-Washing

★ Large tub
★ Water and hose
★ Pet brush
★ Pet shampoo
★ Old towels
★ Pet treat

## Skills Learned

✔ Responsibility and running a business
✔ Writing skills and reading development
✔ Cognitive development/ problem solving/cause and effect
✔ Animal studies
✔ Fine and gross motor skills
✔ Social interaction
✔ Money management and math skills

## What to Do

### Pet-Sitting and Pet-Walking

1. Decide what kinds of animals you'd like to sit, such as cats, dogs, birds, rats, hamsters, guineas pigs, rabbits, and so on. Think about what pets you'd rather not sit, such as snakes, ant farms, and elephants.

2. Get a book from the library or bookstore on how to take care of the pets. Read the information and make notes on the important points.

3. Think about how much you want to charge for your services. You might charge $2 to $5 a sitting or charge by the hour, such as from $.50 to $2 per hour.

4. Think about when you are available to sit, perhaps weekends only, days, evenings, or any time.

5. Design flyers for your business. Draw them up on colorful paper so they're attractive and easy to read. Include the following information on your flyer:

   Your first name (no last name for your protection)

   Your phone number

   What kinds of pets you'll take care of

   What your services include, such as pet-sitting, petwalking, pet-washing, and so on

   What you charge (or you can negotiate that in person)

   When you're available (weekends only, for example)

6. Post the flyers around the neighborhood or hand them out to individual neighbors.

7. When you get a call, set up an appointment to meet with the pet owner to discuss her needs and your services. Pay special attention to the pet during your meeting and try to get to know it while you're there.

8. If you get the job, be sure to be on time (even a few minutes early) and do the job well. While you pet-sit, you might play with the pet, take it for a walk, go to the park, feed it, or even give it a bath (perhaps for an extra charge).

9. Collect your money after the job is done and thank the pet owners for hiring you. If you did a good job, you'll probably be asked to pet-sit again.

### Pet-Washing

1. Find a friend to help you, if possible, since pet-washing can be a tricky task.

2. Go outside and fill a large tub with warm water.

3. Brush the pet thoroughly to remove excess dirt and hair.

4. Put the pet in the wash and hold onto him securely, without hurting him. If the pet has a collar, hold onto that. Talk to the pet the whole time you're washing him to make him feel secure.

5. Squirt a little pet shampoo onto the back of the pet's neck and massage it in, adding water to make it sudsy. Spread the suds all over the pet, being careful not to get it in his face and eyes.

6. Turn the hose on low and rinse the shampoo from the pet. Massage his fur as you rinse him to get all the suds out. Be sure you get *all* the shampoo out.

7. Dry your pet thoroughly, using several old towels. Give him a chance to shake off the water after you have dried him a little so the water doesn't spray all over you.

8. Praise your pet and give him a treat for when you have completed the task.

## More Fun

Offer to put on a party for a pet and invite some other pets to join in the fun. Make special pet treats, play some games, and give the pets a play toy as a favor.

# 12
# Nature Fun

Plant a Garden

Nature Scavenger Hunt

Rock Star

Crystal Garden

Grass Head

Terrarium

# Plant a Garden

Ages 3 to 12

Summer is the perfect time to plant a garden. It will keep you entertained—and maybe fed—all summer long.

## Materials

★ Variety of seeds, such as carrots, beans, and corn
★ Popsicle sticks
★ Potting soil
★ Water from hose or watering can
★ Hoe and trowel

## Skills Learned

✔ Scientific properties
✔ Nature studies
✔ Cognitive skills/problem solving/cause and effect
✔ Reading comprehension
✔ Writing skills

## What to Do

1. Find a sunny area of dirt for your garden, roughly 6 or 8 feet square.
2. Clear away the weeds.

3. Loosen the soil by digging it up with a hoe or shovel until it's crumbly, about a foot deep.

4. Spread potting soil over the dirt.

5. Buy seeds and read the directions on the backs of the packs, which explain when, how deep, and how far apart to plant your seeds.

6. Using the hoe, dig out a narrow row about 3 inches deep (or whatever depth the package directions tell you).

7. Plant the seeds in the rows and cover them with the dirt.

8. Mark the rows by stapling each seed packet to one end of a Popsicle stick and then inserting the sticks into the dirt so you'll know what you planted and where.

9. Water the seeds gently—don't overwater them.

10. Make a chart to keep track of what you planted and when. Then check your garden each day to see if there are signs of growth. Record on your chart any progress you see.

11. Pull out smaller plants that are too close together so the main plants won't get choked out by too many plants.

12. Check the seed packets for information about when to pick your vegetables.

## Safety Tips

★ Be careful with the hoe and shovel— they have sharp ends that can cause injury.
★ Don't use poisonous sprays on your plants.

# Nature Scavenger Hunt

Ages 3 to 12

You see items in nature every day, but do you really notice them? Now is your chance to find what you're looking for.

## Materials

★ Paper and pencil
★ Large bag with a handle
★ Magnifying glass (optional)
★ Large sheet of posterboard
★ Glue
★ Colored markers

## Skills Learned

✔ Observation and classification skills
✔ Writing and charting skills
✔ Nature studies

## What to Do

1. Write a list of 10 items to look for in nature, or have a parent write the list for you. Include such things as:

   | | |
   |---|---|
   | Yellow leaf | Feather |
   | Smooth stone | Seed pod |
   | Pinecone | Snail shell |
   | Y-shaped twig | Acorn |
   | White flower | Weed |

2. See if you can find all the items on the list. (Be careful not to pick up anything poisonous, like poison oak or poison ivy!)

**3.** Glue the items on posterboard.

**4.** Mark where you found the items.

**5.** Write down how long it took you to find all the items.

## More Fun

Race with a friend to see who can find all the items first. Or make it a Trash Scavenger Hunt and try to find 10 different trash items in nature, such as a gum wrapper, an aluminum can, a candy wrapper, a napkin, a paper bag, and so on. That way you'll be helping to keep the planet clean while you play. Or turn the game into Nature Bingo and find items you've drawn on a Bingo card.

# Rock Star

Ages 3 to 12

It's easy to start a rock collection—there are rocks all over the place. And everywhere you go, you'll find more rocks to add to your collection.

**Materials**

★ Rocks

★ Book about rocks

★ Shoebox

★ Paper and pencil

★ Colored markers

**Skills Learned**

✔ Observation and classification skills

✔ Nature and environmental studies

✔ Writing and charting skills

## What to Do

1. Head for your backyard, neighborhood, or a local park. Also try streams, lakes, excavation sites, and nature areas (first be sure they allow you to take rocks).

2. Collect a variety of rocks, making sure each one is different. Place them in the shoebox.

3. When you get back home, set your collection on the table so you can examine each rock.

4. Look at your rock book and see if you can identify each rock.

5. Sort the rocks into one of the following rock categories:

   *Sedimentary rocks*—made when mud, sand, and minerals settle and harden, usually found where land was underwater

   *Metamorphic rocks*—changed by pressure or heat, usually found where land has buckled or rolled and broken open

   *Igneous rocks*—volcanic rock, usually found where land was once near a volcano

6. Categorize the rocks as many different ways as you can, such as:

   Smooth versus rough

   Shiny versus dull

   Round versus square

   Light versus heavy

   Solid versus porous (full of holes)

   Color

### More Fun

Visit a rock shop to see what rocks you still need to find. Keep adding to your collection throughout the summer.

7. Note the place where you found the rock. See if you find similar rocks in other areas and note that also.

# Crystal Garden

Ages 7 to 12

You don't need a deep dark cave to grow your own crystal garden—just a few common items that combine magically.

## Materials
★ Coal chunks
★ Brick pieces
★ Shallow bowl or dish about 6 inches wide
★ Mixing bowl
★ Salt—not iodized
★ Liquid bluing
★ Water
★ Ammonia
★ Food coloring
★ Paper and pencil

## Skills Learned
✔ Scientific properties
✔ Cause and effect
✔ Writing and charting skills

## What to Do
1. Break up coal or brick into pieces the size of walnuts.
2. Put the pieces in the center of the shallow dish.
3. Carefully mix 4 tablespoons salt, 4 tablespoons bluing, 4 tablespoons water, and 1 tablespoon ammonia in mixing bowl.
4. Pour the mixture carefully over the broken pieces, leaving a few pieces uncovered.
5. Drip a few drops of food coloring on the center pieces.

**6.** Set the bowl aside so it won't be disturbed.

**7.** Check the bowl in a few hours and see if there's been any change.

**8.** Record the changes and the time.

**9.** Make another bowl of crystals, but this time leave out the ammonia. Cover the broken pieces completely with the solution—and keep them covered for two weeks by adding more solution every few days. Then stop adding solution and see what happens.

## Safety Tips

★ Be careful with the ammonia and don't inhale it.
★ Wash your hands after handling the materials.

# Grass Head

Ages 7 to 12

Make your own funny fuzz heads and watch them grow their own personalities.

## Materials

★ Old nylon stocking
★ 32-ounce plastic soda bottle
★ Scissors
★ Grass seeds
★ Potting soil
★ Watering can
★ Permanent black or colored markers
★ Fabric scraps

## Skills Learned

✔ Reading and following directions
✔ Nature studies
✔ Creative and imaginative thinking

## What to Do

1. Find an old nylon stocking and cut off one leg so it's about 3 feet long, or use a knee-high stocking.
2. Cut both ends off the soda bottle to form a tube.
3. Slip the nylon over the bottle so it's completely covered to form a foundation for the body.
4. Sprinkle 2 to 3 tablespoons of lawn seeds into the nylon and shake them down into the toe.
5. Fill the rest of the nylon with potting soil and press it down firmly.
6. Carefully slip the bottle from between the nylon and the potting soil and tightly tie off the open end of the nylon.
7. Turn the dirt-filled nylon upright, with the tie at the bottom and the grass seed at the top, and set it in a bowl to keep it upright.
8. Draw a funny face on the top half of the nylon with the permanent markers.

9. Tie some fabric around the bottom half to make an outfit for the body.

10. Sprinkle a little water on top of the head and set it in a sunny place.

11. Give your Grass Head a name, water it every day, and watch its "hair" grow from the grass seed.

> **More Fun**
>
> Make a bunch of Grass Heads to represent your whole family.

# Terrarium

Ages 7 to 12

Bring a little nature indoors and enjoy a miniature garden in your own bedroom.

## Materials

★ Goldfish bowl, small aquarium tank, or large glass jar
★ Potting soil
★ Small plants, such as cactus, ferns, flowers, herbs, and so on
★ Watering can and water

## Skills Learned

✔ Nature studies
✔ Cognitive skills/cause and effect
✔ Scientific properties
✔ Writing and record keeping

## What to Do

1. Find a clear glass or plastic container to build your terrarium.

2. Spread a layer of potting soil on the bottom of the container, about 3 inches deep.

3. Carefully transfer plants into the potting soil, press the roots gently into the dirt, and cover the top of the roots with more potting soil so the roots are completely covered (but make sure the plant is above the dirt).

4. Water the garden with your watering can until the soil is just moist, not soaked.

5. Set the terrarium by a sunny window.

6. Record the date, the type of plants you used, and how much water you poured, and describe the size, condition, and details of the plants.

7. Water the plants each day and note the details of the plants in your record book.

## More Fun

Buy a Venus Flycatcher, plant it in your terrarium, and feed it flies. Watch how the plant takes in its food.

# 13
# Nighttime Fun

Camp Snacks
Lights Out!
Nighttime Noises
Searchlight
Flashlight Fun
Campfire Cookout
Tent Time

# Camp Snacks

Ages 3 to 12

When you can't build a fire, prepare a few snacks ahead of time to take with you on the trail or into the tent.

## Materials

### Banana Bites
★ Bananas
★ Knife
★ Cookie sheet
★ Vegetable cooking spray

### Trail and Tent Mix
★ 1 cup each raisins and/or other dried fruit, small pretzels, cereal, nuts, seeds, coconut

### Hot Chocolate to Go
★ 2 cups powdered milk
★ ½ cup sweetened chocolate drink mix
★ Cup and spoon

## Skills Learned
✔ Following directions
✔ Planning and being prepared
✔ Independence
✔ Good nutrition

## What to Do

### Banana Bites
1. Slice bananas into thin circles.
2. Spray vegetable spray on the cookie sheet.
3. Place banana slices on the sheet in a single layer.

**4.** Bake at 150 degrees for 2 hours with the oven door open an inch.

**5.** Turn and bake another 2 hours (again with oven door open an inch), until firm.

**6.** Cool and store in plastic baggie.

### Trail and Tent Mix

**1.** Mix raisins, pretzels, cereal, chopped nuts, seeds, coconut, and whatever else you like in a large bowl or large bag.

**2.** Pour individual amounts into small baggies and seal until snack time.

### Hot Chocolate to Go

**1.** Pour powdered milk and chocolate drink mix into a large bowl or bag and mix well.

**2.** Pour into large plastic bag and seal it.

**3.** Fill a cup ¾ full with hot water.

**4.** Add 2 heaping table-spoons of chocolate mix and stir.

> **More Fun**
>
> Think up some other snacks you like and see if you can adapt them into good outdoors or camping food.

# Lights Out!

Ages 3 to 12

Spend the evening with the lights out—and see what happens in the dark.

## Materials

★ Flashlight
★ Candles
★ Food
★ Books
★ Objects to find

## Skills Learned

✔ Problem solving
✔ Cognitive skills and creative thinking
✔ Social skills
✔ Reading skills

## What to Do

1. Choose a night for "Lights Out!" and gather the family.
2. Do all your normal nighttime tasks, but do them in the dark, using only flashlights or candles for light. Here are some things you might try in the dark:

   Take a bath.

   Cook and eat dinner.

   Do your homework.

   Clean your room.

3. When you're finished with your normal tasks, have some fun in the dark:

   Play a board game.

   Read a book.

   Search for hidden objects in the room using your flashlight.

   Play Hide and Seek with the flashlights.

   Lie in bed, shine your flashlights on the ceiling and chase each other's lights.

   Play Follow the Light by shin-

### Safety Tips

★ Be careful around the candles so you don't set the house on fire!
★ Watch where you go in the dark so you don't bump into something and hurt yourself!

ing it around the floor and having another person try to follow where it goes.

Instead of just turning off the lights, don't use any electricity all night long. See how well you get along and what you miss the most.

# Nighttime Noises

Ages 3 to 12

Do you ever wonder what all those night noises are? See if you can name them all.

## Materials

★ Cassette tape recorder and tape
★ Noises

## Skills Learned

✔ Creative and imaginative thinking
✔ Cognitive skills/cause and effect
✔ Classification skills

## What to Do

1. Set your tape recorder outside, turn it on, and record the sounds of the night.

2. When you're in your tent the next night, play the tape recorder and see if you can identify all the sounds you hear. You might hear birds,

### More Fun

Listen to the sounds live and try to guess what they are. Or make up your own sounds and see if another player can guess the sound.

crickets, frogs, wind, water, owls, dogs, and other sounds of nature.

3. Play the tape again and make up a story to go with each sound.

# Searchlight

Ages 3 to 12

How good is your night vision? Find out with a game of Searchlight. Turn your flashlights on.

## Materials
★ Flashlights
★ Darkness
★ 10 or so objects to find

## Skills Learned
✔ Cognitive skills/problem solving
✔ Visual and scanning skills
✔ Social interaction

## What to Do

1. Choose one person to hide 10 or so objects outside or in a room in the house. Make sure they are hidden but still easy to find.
2. Give everyone a flashlight.
3. Go outside into the dark, or turn off all the lights in the house (or in one room) and race to find as many objects as you can, using your flashlights.
4. The player who finds the most wins the game and gets to hide the objects the next time.

**Safety Tip**

Be careful you don't trip and fall in the dark or bump into something!

# Flashlight Fun

Ages 3 to 12*

*Note: Light Language is recommended for ages 7 to 12.*

There's nothing to be afraid of in the dark—especially when you have plenty of flashlights to play with.

## Materials

★ Flashlight for each player
★ Black paper
★ Scissors
★ Tape

## Skills Learned

✔ Visual perception
✔ Creative and imaginative thinking
✔ Social interaction

## What to Do

### Flashlight Flight

1. Have one player shine the flashlight on the tent ceiling and move it around.
2. Have the other players try to catch the light with their own flashlights.
3. Take turns moving and chasing the light.

### Follow the Flashlight

1. Have one player shine her light on the ceiling and move it around.
2. Have the others try to follow the leader light as it moves around.
3. Take turns leading and following the flashlight.

### Star Light

1. Cut out a circle the size of the flashlight lens.
2. Cut out a star shape in the center of the circle.

3. Tape the black circle onto the flashlight lens.
4. Turn on the light and shine it on the ceiling to see the star shape appear.

### Light Language

1. Learn Morse code (see Resources).
2. Talk to each other by turning the light on and off using Morse Code.

## More Fun

Use the flashlight to make hand shadows on the wall. Have players follow the light beam outside as you shine it around the ground. Think up some other games you can play with your flashlight.

# Campfire Cookout

Ages 7 to 12

Half the fun of camping out is cooking out. Get your parents help to fire up the cooking flame and try some of these campfire treats.

## Materials
### Make Fire
★ Hibachi or large rocks
★ Charcoal
★ Lighter fluid
★ Matches

### Supper on a Stick
★ Long stick or wire coat hanger
★ Cut-up hot dog or other meats
★ Cut-up veggies such as zucchini, bell pepper, cherry tomatoes, or small precooked potatoes
★ Pineapple chunks
★ Brown and serve rolls

### S'mores
★ Graham crackers
★ Chocolate bars
★ Marshmallows

## Skills Learned
✔ Following instructions
✔ Measurement and math
✔ Scientific properties
✔ Cognitive skills/cause and effect/problem solving
✔ Planning and carrying out plans

## What to Do
### Make Fire
1. Ask your parents to help you light the hibachi or make a campfire by arranging large rocks around in a circle.
2. Place charcoal in the center in a pyramid shape.
3. Douse with a little lighter fluid, but be extremely careful!
4. Carefully light a match and toss it into the center of the charcoal.

5. Give the fire about 15 minutes to get hot enough for cooking. If the fire goes out, ask a parent to relight it for you.

### Supper on a Stick

1. Cut up or prepare meat, veggies, pineapple, and rolls and push them onto the stick or coat hanger.
2. Hold the stick over the fire or coals until the meat changes color, the veggies are moist and tender, and the rolls are browned and cooked inside.
3. Carefully remove the food from the stick onto a paper plate—or eat it right from the stick.

### S'mores

1. Set a graham cracker on a paper plate.
2. Place a chocolate bar on top of the graham cracker.
3. Have another graham cracker ready.
4. Stick a couple of marshmallows onto a long stick or straightened coat hanger.
5. Hold the marshmallows over the coals, about an inch or two away, and keep turning them until they become light brown. Don't let them catch on fire—unless you liked them burned!
6. When the marshmallows are warm and gooshy, place them on the chocolate-covered graham cracker.
7. Place the other graham cracker on top and press down to help melt the chocolate with the marshmallow, then gently pull out the stick.
8. Enjoy your s'more, then make some more!

## Safety Tips

★ Be extremely careful around the fire so you don't get burned.
★ Make sure the fire is completely out before you go to bed.

# Tent Time

Ages 7 to 12

If you don't have a real tent, here are some ways to make your own tent—and some ideas for what to put inside.

## Materials

★ Rope
★ Tarp or thick blanket or sleeping bag
★ 1 or 2 trees
★ Tent pegs or heavy rocks
★ Radio, comics, water bottle, flashlight, snacks, games, and cards

## Skills Learned

✔ Creative and imaginative thinking
✔ Cognitive skills/problem solving
✔ Independence and competence

## What to Do

1. If there are 2 sturdy trees relatively close together in your backyard, tie a rope to both of them, stretched taut, about 3 to 4 feet from the ground.

2. If you have only 1 tree, tie the rope to the tree about 5 feet from the ground and secure the other end of the rope to the ground with a tent peg.

3. Drape the tarp or blanket over the rope to form a tent.

4. Secure the tarp to the ground with tent pegs or large rocks on the outside.

5. Lay sleeping bags on the ground under the tarp and head into your tent.

**Safety Tip**

Make sure the tent pegs are secure, and be careful not to trip over them in the middle of the night in the dark!

# 14
# Outdoor Adventures

Bird Feeder

Shadows and Stories

ABC Scavenger Hunt

Go Fly a Kite

Adopt a Neighborhood

Clock Box

Sunlight Photos

Tree Fort

Backyard Swing

# Bird Feeder

Ages 3 to 12

Welcome the birds to your yard and see how many you can attract to your restaurant in the sky.

## Materials
★ Half-gallon milk carton
★ Scissors
★ String
★ 1-foot-long dowel or stick
★ Birdseed, sunflower seeds, nuts, bread crumbs

## Skills Learned
✔ Nature studies
✔ Cognitive skills/classification skills
✔ Writing skills
✔ Reading and vocabulary

## What to Do
1. Rinse and dry the milk carton.
2. Cut out one side, leaving a 2-inch bottom to hold the food inside.
3. Poke a hole at the top of the carton with scissors and insert string to tie to the tree.
4. Poke 2 holes, 1 on either side at the bottom, and insert a dowel or stick through the holes to make a perch.

## More Fun
See if you can recognize the same birds each day by noting the details of their features and feathers. Give each bird a name if you like. Make a bird bath so the birds can clean up after they eat. Fill a pan with water and set it on a picnic table, tree stump, or some kind of pedestal so the birds can enjoy their bath.

5. Tie bird feeder to a sturdy tree limb.
6. Fill the bottom with birdseed.
7. Make a chart to record the types and numbers of birds that visit your bird feeder.

# Shadows and Stories

Ages 3 to 12

Use the sun to guide your drawings, then trace the shadows and create your own costumed characters.

## Materials
★ Sidewalk chalk
★ Pavement

## Skills Learned
✔ Creative and imaginative thinking
✔ Storytelling
✔ Writing skills
✔ Reading skills

## What to Do
1. Have a friend strike a pose in the sun to create an interesting shadow.
2. Draw the outline of the friend's shadow created by the sun using the sidewalk chalk.
3. Add details to the outline, such as a face, hands, feet, and body marks.
4. Add a costume to the body, such as a super hero, cartoon character, monster, or career uniform.

5. Add some accessories, such as a magic wand, a funny hat, spiders and bats, or a doctor's stethoscope.

6. Repeat until everyone has at least one shadow character. Make as many characters as you like.

7. Name the characters and write a story about them using the chalk.

8. Make the same character, but pose it in different ways. Then write a caption for each pose, like a giant comic strip.

**Safety Tip**

Draw your characters on the sidewalk, patio, driveway, or empty parking lot, not the street, or you might get run over by a car!

# ABC Scavenger Hunt

Ages 7 to 12

Can you find the alphabet on your scavenger hunt? There are plenty of letters out there to find.

## Materials
★ Paper bag or paper and pencil
★ Timer or watch

## Skills Learned
✔ Cognitive skills/ classification
✔ Social interaction and cooperation
✔ Visual skills
✔ Gross motor development/ exercise

## What to Do

1. Divide into teams.
2. Get paper bags for each player, or paper and pencil instead.
3. Set the timer for 30 minutes, or note the time on the watch, and begin the game.
4. Go outdoors and find as many items as you can that begin with each letter of the alphabet. For example, find an ant for A, a berry for B, a candy wrapper for C, and so on.
5. You can either collect the items in the paper bag or write them down on paper.
6. At the end of 30 minutes, gather together and see how many items each team found.
7. The team that finds items representing the most alphabet letters wins the game.

> **More Fun**
>
> Don't set a time limit. Instead, keep playing until one team finds all the alphabet items first.

# Go Fly a Kite

Ages 7 to 12

Make your own kite, then sail it up in the summer sky and see how high it will fly.

## Materials

★ 1 wooden dowel, ¼ inch in diameter, 30 inches long
★ 1 wooden dowel, ¼ inch in diameter, 24 inches long
★ Knife
★ Ruler
★ String—at least 3 yards long
★ Electrical tape
★ Kite string
★ Scissors
★ Kite covering—30- by 24-inch piece of fabric, such as old sheets, fabric remnants, brown package wrap, plastic garbage bags, or "ripstop" fabric available at the fabric store
★ Kite tail materials, such as ribbons, fabric scraps, or tissue paper

## Skills Learned

✔ Cognitive skills/problem solving/cause and effect
✔ Fine and gross motor skills/exercise
✔ Competence and self-confidence
✔ Social skills
✔ Scientific properties
✔ Math and measurement

## What to Do

1. Soak the wood in water to make it flexible.
2. Carve a V notch at each end of both dowels.
3. Measure from one end along the 30-inch dowel and mark off 8 inches.
4. Measure from one end of the 24-inch dowel and mark off 12 inches.

**5.** Cross the pieces at right angles to form a cross at the two marks.

**6.** With string, tie the dowels together where they cross.

**7.** Add some glue for extra strength and let it dry completely, then reinforce it with tape.

**8.** Run a piece of kite string through the notches around the outside of the dowels to form a frame.

**9.** Put electrical tape around the ends to keep the string secure.

**10.** Measure and cut kite covering from fabric, allowing a seam margin 2 inches larger than the frame.

**11.** Lay the covering over the frame, fold the seam allowance around the dowels, and glue or tape it closed.

**12.** Poke 2 holes diagonally in the center of the kite, on either side of the dowels.

**13.** Thread a short piece of string loosely through the holes and around the cross made by the dowels to form a loop.

**14.** Attach your kite string to this loop on the side of the fabric opposite the crossbar.

**15.** Make a tail that has a length 6 times longer than the width of the kite, and tie on ribbons, fabric, or tissue paper.

**16.** Go fly a kite!

## Safety Tips

★ Be careful when cutting the notches, or have a parent help you.

★ Don't fly your kite in an electrical (lightning) storm, or you may get shocked!

★ If your kite gets tangled in wires, let it go and tell your parents so they can alert the electric company.

# Adopt a Neighborhood

Ages 7 to 12

Maybe you've seen the signs on the freeways that say "Highway Adopted by Big Corporation." Have you ever thought about adopting your neighborhood?

## Materials

★ Large bag with a handle
★ Old fork
★ Broomstick or long stick
★ Electrical tape
★ Posterboard
★ Markers
★ Paper and pencil
★ Garden gloves

## Skills Learned

✔ Nature and environment
✔ Social responsibility
✔ Helping others
✔ Classification skills
✔ Writing and recording

## What to Do

1. Get a large bag, preferably one with a handle you can wear on your shoulder or arm.
2. Tape an old fork to the end of a broomstick using the electrical tape. Make sure the prongs stick out beyond the end of the broomstick and that the fork handle is securely attached so it doesn't wobble or fall off.
3. Use posterboard to create a sign that reads, "Neighborhood Adopted by (Your Name)."
4. Tape the sign to a pole on your street.
5. Put on your garden gloves and go around the neighborhood collecting as much litter as you can find.

**6.** Use the broomstick to stab papers and put them in your shoulder bag.

**7.** If you can't stab the litter, just pick it up and put it in your bag.

**8.** When you get back home, sort the litter out in the yard to see what you have. (Keep your gloves on!)

**9.** Record the items on paper and count them.

**10.** Clean up your neighborhood each week, and see if the amount and type of litter changes.

**11.** Have a friend join you in your litter collection and race to find the most. See how many items match and how many are different. Record the most unusual finds in your collection.

## Safety Tips

★ Be sure to wear your gloves so you don't get your hands dirty or pick up any germs from the litter.
★ Be careful with the broomstick when stabbing the litter so you don't stab your toe!

# Clock Box

### Ages 7 to 12

Here's a way to tell time without a watch. Just use the sun to mark the hours so you can keep track of your day.

## Materials

★ Shoebox

★ String

★ Tape

★ Colorful markers

## Skills Learned

✔ Telling time

✔ Math and measurement skills

✔ Cognitive skills/cause and effect

## What to Do

1. Remove the lid of the shoebox.
2. Cut the string a few inches longer than the length of the shoebox.
3. Tie a bead to the center of the string.
4. Stretch the string across the top of the box, lengthwise, and center it.
5. Tape the ends of the strings to the sides of the box, to keep the string taut across the top.
6. Set the box in the sun with the ends facing north and south.
7. Every hour check the box to see where the bead shadow is, and mark the time with a colored marker.
8. After you've marked each hour of daylight, you can use the box each day to tell what time it is.

## More Fun

Use your clock box all summer, but check the time at the end of the season to see if the marks are still accurate. Has the time changed? (It will change if the time changes to daylight savings time.)

# Sunlight Photos

Ages 7 to 12

You don't need a camera to take a sunlight photograph. But you'll need special paper to make these magical prints.

## Materials

★ Nature items, such as leaves, flowers, feathers, and so on
★ Light-sensitive paper, available at the hobby or photo store
★ Water
★ Sunny day
★ Permanent markers

## Skills Learned

✔ Cognitive skills/cause and effect
✔ Scientific properties
✔ Nature studies

## What to Do

1. Make sure it's a sunny day.
2. Collect some objects from nature that you think will make interesting pictures in outline form.
3. Read the instructions on the light-sensitive paper before you begin.
4. In a darkened room, place the photo paper on a cookie sheet.
5. Arrange the nature items on the photo paper to make an interesting picture or design.
6. Take the tray with the paper and nature items out into the sun.
7. Time the exposure for 5 minutes.

**8.** Remove the items from the paper and dip the paper in water.

**9.** Lay out the paper to dry.

**10.** When the paper is dry, add details to enhance the design with permanent markers, if you like.

**More Fun**

Lay your hand on the paper to make a hand print, then think up ways to make creative pictures from the hand print.

# Tree Fort

Ages 7 to 12

Create your own home away from home where you can hang with friends or spend time by yourself.

## Materials

★ *Wood*—boards, sheets, scraps
★ *Cloth*—old sheets, blankets, fabric lengths
★ *Furniture*—mats, pillows, stools
★ *Accessories*—camp light, radio, utensils, tools
★ *Fun stuff*—games, books, toys
★ *Extras*—pictures, decorations, cozy comforts, food
★ *Tools*—hammer and nails, duct tape, stapler

## Skills Learned

✔ Planning and carrying out plans
✔ Creative and imaginative thinking
✔ Cognitive skills/problem solving
✔ Competence and independence

## What to Do

1. Find a spot for your tree house, such as a large tree, a fence corner, a vacant patch of the yard, some underbrush, or another secluded area that could be turned into a fort.

2. Ask your parents for permission to build a fort and then start planning how you want it to look. Think about the area you've chosen for your fort and make sure it's a good place to construct it. Are there bushes or trees to use for camouflage? Is it far from the house? Are you disturbing anything in the yard that your parents might not appreciate?

3. Collect wood scraps and materials to create the fort. Use wood panels or old sheets for walls and secure them with hanger and nails, duct tape, or staples.

4. Add some furniture so it's comfortable to sit or lie down in your fort.

5. Bring in some accessories to add to your fort, as well as some fun stuff, and any extras you think you'd like to have.

6. Invite friends to help you build the fort or to join you inside when it's complete.

7. If your friends aren't around, use the fort for quiet time to think, read, or get away from your siblings if they're driving you crazy.

### Safety Tips

★ Bring only food that is wrapped so it won't attract animals or ants.

★ Be sure your structure is safe so no one gets hurt or falls off.

# Backyard Swing

Ages 10 to 12

Make your own comfy tire swing so you can rock and relax in the hot and humid weather.

## Materials

★ Old worn tire, wide enough for you to sit in
★ Heavy-duty shears or strong knife
★ 2 pieces of heavy rope, 10 feet each
★ Tree
★ Old pillow

## Skills Learned

✔ Cognitive skills
✔ Fine and gross motor development
✔ Math and measurement
✔ Competence and independence

## What to Do

1. Get an old tire from the tire store, large enough for you to fit inside when you sit in it.
2. With your parent's supervision or assistance, cut off the center parts of the tire using shears or a strong knife, leaving the outside rim to sit in.
3. Cut out 2 small holes at the top of the backrest to hold the rope.
4. Tie a long piece of heavy rope to a strong tree limb.

## Safety Tips

★ Get a parent's help when you cut the tire with shears or a knife.
★ Make sure the tree limb is sturdy and strong so the swing doesn't come crashing down.

5. Thread it through one of the small holes and tie it off securely.

6. Repeat for the other side.

7. Place an old pillow inside the tire seat to make it comfortable.

8. Get in, swing away, and make your own breeze.

# 15
# Play with Pals

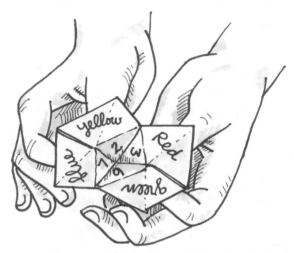

Blanket Buildings
Deejay Dance
Hose Phone
Carnival Time
Giant Board Game
Rock Candy
Secret Codes
Summer "School"
Cootie Catcher

# Blanket Buildings

Ages 3 to 9

Turn your family room into a fort and tunnel your way into a whole new world.

## Materials

★ Room to use for your fort
★ Blankets, sheets, and large towels
★ Extra chairs, tables, and benches
★ Heavy books
★ Accessories for your fort, such as flashlights, games, pillows, books, and so on

## Skills Learned

✔ Creative and imaginative thinking
✔ Cognitive skills/problem solving
✔ Social interaction
✔ Independence and competence

## What to Do

1. Get permission from your parents to turn a room into a fort.
2. Collect as many blankets, sheets, and large towels as you can find.
3. Bring in a few extra chairs, tables, and benches and set them around the room where there's no furniture.
4. Spread the blankets, sheets, and towels over all the furniture to make a fort. Secure the blankets by placing books on top of them if necessary.
5. Create an opening at one end of the fort so you can get in and out easily. You might hang a towel over a chair that

you've turned side-
ways so you have
to crawl through
to get inside, or
make a tunnel out
of chairs.

**6.** Bring in a few
accessories, such
as the ones
mentioned, and move
into your fort.

### Safety Tips

★ Be careful that the books don't fall on top of you while you're in the fort.
★ Don't bring anything into the fort that might be dangerous, such as a hot lamp.
★ Don't bring in any food that might attract ants.

**7.** Be sure you clean it all up when you're finished playing so you get your room back.

# Deejay Dance

### Ages 3 to 12

Spin some tunes and get the kids rocking to the music
by making up your own new dance steps.

### Materials

★ Cassette player or boom-
box
★ Music tapes or CDs
★ Radio

### Skills Learned

✔ Gross motor development/
exercise
✔ Social interaction
✔ Creative and imaginative
thinking
✔ Cognitive skills

## What to Do

1. Clear an area for the dance floor. An uncarpeted area works best.

2. Choose some music to dance to. Try a variety of tunes and beats, such as rap, pop, salsa, reggae, even classical and slow tunes.

3. Turn on the first song and make up a new dance to the beat and tune.

4. Have the others follow along.

5. When a new song comes on, choose another dancer to create a new dance.

6. Keep inventing new dances to go with each new song.

7. Review the songs and see if you can remember all the new dance steps.

### More Fun

Instead of playing your own tunes, have someone spin the radio dial and change your dance steps to match each new song that comes along. Keep the music spinning and the dancers hopping.

# Hose Phone

Ages 3 to 12

Make your own intercom system that goes from room to room, or even from house to house.

## Materials

★ Garden hose, as long as you can find
★ 2 large funnels (with one end small enough to fit inside a garden hose)
★ Duct tape

## Skills Learned

✔ Cognitive skills/cause and effect
✔ Scientific properties
✔ Social interaction
✔ Language and communication skills

## What to Do

1. Insert one funnel into each end of the garden hose.
2. Tape the funnels to the hose ends with duct tape to secure them.
3. Stretch out the hose and go into two rooms or around a corner so you can't see each other.
4. Talk into the funnel when you want to say something.
5. Listen by holding the funnel up to your ear to hear the other person speaking.
6. Take turns talking and listening.

### More Fun

Think up ways you can use your Hose Phone for communicating. Try singing, playing music, tapping out a code, making noises, and listening to TV or the radio from a distance.

# Carnival Time

Ages 7 to 12

Put on your own carnival, right there in your yard, court, or driveway, and invite the neighborhood to try their luck at the "carny" games.

## Materials

★ Squirt guns
★ Paper cups
★ Cardboard boxes
★ Rolled-up socks
★ Paint or markers

## Skills Learned

✔ Cognitive skills/problem solving
✔ Planning and carrying out plans
✔ Writing skills
✔ Imaginative and creative thinking
✔ Social skills
✔ Time management and scheduling

## What to Do

1. Gather a few friends and begin to plan your carnival.
2. Decide what day and what time to hold the event.
3. Make up posters to advertise your carnival and tape them to poles or trees around the neighborhood.
4. Make flyers to put in neighborhood mailboxes.
5. Plan the games and activities. You might include the following:

   *Shooting Gallery*
   Set up paper cups along a fence or picnic table.

Have players try to shoot them over using squirt guns.

*Clown Toss*

Cut a circle out of a large cardboard box.

Paint or color a clown face around the circle, making the circle the wide-open mouth of the clown.

Ball up some old socks and have players try to toss the sock balls through the mouth hole.

*Penny Plates*

Set out some plates on a picnic table or other table.

Give the players 10 pennies to try to toss onto the plates.

Award the winners with small prizes.

Have a face-painting booth and paint the little kids' faces.

Sell lemonade, cookies, and cupcakes to the hungry crowd.

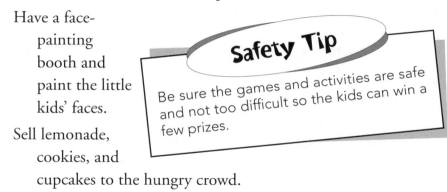

**Safety Tip**

Be sure the games and activities are safe and not too difficult so the kids can win a few prizes.

# Giant Board Game

Ages 7 to 12

Super-size and bring to life your favorite board games, then play the game using yourself as a game piece.

## Materials

★ Room to play in
★ 25 sheets of colored construction paper
★ 10 pieces of furniture, including couch, chairs, benches, and pillows
★ Colorful markers
★ 1 die

## Skills Learned

✔ Writing skills
✔ Cognitive development/ cause and effect/problem solving
✔ Fine and gross motor skills
✔ Creative and imaginative thinking
✔ Social skills

## What to Do

1. Set some extra furniture and pillows in your play room, arranged in a circle.
2. On 20 sheets of construction paper, write different tasks to perform, such as "Hop on one foot ten times without falling," "Say the alphabet backwards," "Recite a poem in duck language," "Make a funny face and get someone to laugh," "Burp your name," "Recite everyone's phone numbers," and so on.
3. Write "Start" on one sheet of paper and "Winner" on another sheet.
4. Write "Go back to start" on three of the sheets.
5. Mix up the sheets and place them around the room, between pieces of furniture and pillows, each about a foot apart. Put the "Start" and "Winner" sheets next to each other.
6. Roll the die to see who goes first.
7. With all players, beginning at "Start," have the first player roll the die and take the number of steps indicated on the top of the die, moving from paper to paper.

**8.** When a player lands on a paper, he must perform the task written on it to stay on that spot. If he misses the task, he must return to the start.

**9.** If two players land on the same spot, they must race to do the task. That means the player who is already there must perform the task again to keep his space. Whoever finishes it first gets to stay, while the other player must return to the start.

**10.** The person who makes it to the "Winner" spot first wins the game.

## More Fun

Make up your own rules for the game. For example, you might have players move ahead or back a few spaces, answer a trivia question, roll the die to determine which of two players gets to stay on a space, or use index cards to write additional tasks. Or turn your favorite board game, such as Monopoly or Careers, into a Giant Game.

# Rock Candy

Ages 7 to 12

You can make your own candy, as long as you have a sweet tooth—and a little patience.

## Materials

★ Clean glass jar
★ Measuring cup
★ ¼ cup hot water
★ 2 cups sugar
★ Spoon
★ Clean nail, small enough to fit in the jar sideways
★ String
★ Pencil
★ Paper and pencil

## Skills Learned

✔ Cognitive skills/cause and effect
✔ Scientific properties
✔ Following instructions
✔ Math and measurement
✔ Writing and record keeping

## What to Do

1. Pour hot water into the jar.
2. Add sugar, a little at a time, stirring it as you pour.
3. Tie the string to the middle of the pencil.
4. Tie the nail to one end of the string so that when you place the pencil across the top of the jar, the nail hangs down about ½ inch from the bottom of the jar (it shouldn't touch the bottom but should be covered by the sugar mixture).
5. Put the jar in a sunny or warm place.
6. Check the jar every day and make a note in your record book about what is happening inside.
7. Add a few drops of food color after the sugar crystals start to form and see what happens.
8. When you have enough sugar crystals, taste them. Compare them to the taste of sugar.

### Safety Tip

Make sure you use a clean nail and clean jar so that your rocky candy is safe to taste.

# Secret Codes

Ages 7 to 12

Send secret messages to your friends that only those who know the code can read. Here are several ways to code your secret messages.

## Materials
★ Paper and pencil
★ Telephone dial
★ White crayon or invisible markers and decoder pens

## Skills Learned
✔ Writing and language development
✔ Communication skills
✔ Cognitive skills/problem solving
✔ Social interaction

## What to Do

### Alphabackwards Code

1. Write the alphabet on a sheet of paper in a straight line across the top.
2. Now write the alphabet backwards underneath the top line, matching each letter. For example, underneath "A" write "Z," underneath "B" write "Y," and so on.
3. Think of a message you want to write to a friend.
4. Use the reverse alphabet to write your message. For example, the word "You" would read "Blf" in Alphabackwards Code.
5. Mail or give the message to a friend, along with the Alphabackwards decoder, and see if she can figure out your message.
6. Have her write you back using the same code.

### Telephony Code

**1.** Copy the telephone dial or keypad on a piece of paper.

**2.** For the number "1" on the dial, you'll see the letters "A B C." Change the "A" to "1" with a dot on the left side, the "B" to "1" with no dot, and the "C" to "1" with a dot on the right side. If there are 4 letters on a keypad, such as PQRS and WXYZ, put a dot under the second letter (Q and X) and two dots under the third letter (R and Y).

**3.** Repeat for the rest of the alphabet using the numbers on the phone pad as a guide.

**4.** Write a message using the dot and number code.

**5.** Mail or give the message to a friend, along with the Telephony Code, and see if she can figure out the message.

**6.** Have her write you back using the same code.

### Braille

**1.** Learn the Braille alphabet (see Resources), which is a series of specially placed dots that represent the alphabet.

**2.** Write a message using Braille.

**3.** Mail or give the message to a friend, along with a copy of the Braille alphabet, and see if he can figure out the message.

**4.** Have him write you back using Braille.

## More Fun

There are lots of ways to code a message. You might write your message without vowels, or have the reader read only every other letter or the first letters of each sentence, and so on. Use your imagination and creativity to make up your own code that no one will figure out without your decoder.

### Sign Language

1. Learn the American Sign Language manual alphabet (see Resources), which is a series of hand shapes that represent the alphabet.

2. Teach the sign language alphabet to a friend. (Get the book called *Learn to Sign the Fun Way* to help you learn the alphabet.)

3. Practice the sign language alphabet several times, and then practice spelling different words.

4. When you know the alphabet by heart, sign to each other when you don't want anyone to hear your secret conversation.

### Invisible Message

1. Write a message on white paper using a white crayon. Or buy a package of markers that includes an invisible marker and use it to write your message.

2. Mail or give the message to a friend, along with a black crayon or a decoder marker.

3. Have the friend color over the message with the contrasting crayon or marker to read the message.

4. Have him write you back using an invisible crayon or marker that you can color over to read.

# Summer "School"

Ages 7 to 12

Creating your own summer school is a lot more fun than regular school because you get to be the teacher.

## Materials

★ Chairs and tables or large cardboard boxes for desks

★ Paper and pencils

★ Puzzle books/math games/science experiments

★ Word games

★ Red pencil or marker

★ Stick-on stars

## Skills Learned

✔ Reading, writing, and arithmetic

✔ Cognitive skills/problem solving

✔ Math and science studies

✔ Language and vocabulary skills

✔ Leadership/competence

✔ Self-esteem

✔ Organization and planning

✔ Social interaction

## What to Do

1. Set up your classroom with table and chairs or boxes for your students and for yourself as teacher.

2. Organize your school day by breaking it up into different subjects. For example, you might include the following:

| | |
|---|---|
| Pledge of Allegiance | Show and tell |
| Current events | Book reviews |
| Math games | Word games |
| Spelling test | Science experiments |
| Recess | Snack time |
| P.E. or sports | Journal writing |
| Arts and crafts | |

3. Get out paper, pencils, and other materials for your students.

4. Use puzzle books and other game books to create fun projects for your students. After all, you don't want this to be a boring school!

5. When the papers are done, collect them and give everyone a good grade with your red pencil.

6. Once in a while, stick a star on your students' papers and tape them to the wall.

7. Take turns being teacher and students.

### More Fun

Create a Post Office, Grocery Store, Cruise Ship, Hospital, or other career setting and explore the possibilities.

# Cootie Catcher

Ages 7 to 12

Here's the perfect game to play with your friends to find out more about them.

**Materials**
★ Sheet of white construction paper
★ Scissors
★ Fine-tipped colored markers

**Skills Learned**
✔ Social interaction
✔ Creative and imaginative thinking
✔ Fine motor skills
✔ Reading and following directions
✔ Cognitive skills/problem solving

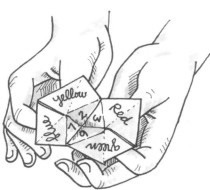

# What to Do

## How to Make

1. Cut out a square of paper about 6" by 6" or 8" by 8".

2. Fold the paper so that two opposite corners meet, and press the fold.

3. Open the paper and refold it so the other two corners meet, and press the fold.

4. Unfold the paper.

5. Fold up one corner until it meets the center of the paper.

6. Repeat for the remaining three corners.

7. Turn the folded paper over and fold all four corners so they meet the center.

8. Turn the paper over and fold the paper in half, along the splits.

9. Unfold and refold the opposite way.

10. Unfold the paper and tuck a thumb and a finger under the tabs on each side to form the Cootie Catcher.

## How to Play

1. On the outside of the catcher, write the name of a color on each flap, such as red, blue, green, and yellow. Use colored markers to match the colors.

2. Turn the Cootie Catcher over and lay it flat.

3. On each of the 8 sections, write the numbers from 1 through 8.

4. Open the flaps and write a fortune on each section, such as "You will become President," "You will be rich," "You will work in the sewer," and so on. Make some of them funny.

5. Close up the Cootie Catcher and reinsert your fingers.

6. Have your friend choose a color from the 4 choices.

7. Count out the letters and open up the Cootie Catcher to the numbers. For example, if your friend chooses "red," count out "3."

8. Have your friend choose a number from the numbers showing.

9. Count off the number and unfold the Cootie Catcher to reveal your friend's fortune. For example, if your friend chooses "8," count off 8 times as you open and close the catcher. When you land at 8, open the flap and read the fortune directly underneath.

10. Take turns telling each other's fortunes.

## More Fun

Make the question more challenging than just colors and numbers, and turn your Cootie Catcher into a Truth-or-Dare Catcher.

# 16
# Sand and Surf

Beach Party

Sand Casting

Sand Painting

Waterscope

Scoop Toss

# Beach Party

Ask the gang to join you at the beach for some fun in
the sun. Surf's up!

## Materials

★ Construction paper
★ Colored markers
★ Beach towels
★ Sand toys
★ Squirt guns
★ Rafts and inner tubes
★ Beach balls and Frisbees
★ Hibachi or barbecue grill
★ Hot dogs or other foods to
   barbecue

## Skills Learned

✔ Making and carrying out
   plans
✔ Organization and time-
   management skills
✔ Social interaction
✔ Writing skills
✔ Creative and imaginative
   thinking

## What to Do

1. Check with your parents to see when would be a good
   time for the beach party.
2. Design your own invitations and send them to your
   guests. You might use beach postcards or glue sand onto
   the cards to make your guests think of the beach.
3. Ask the kids to come with their bathing suits, towels,
   hats, sun lotion, sunglasses, and flip-flops.
4. Gather extra beach towels, sand and beach toys, squirt
   guns or water toys, floaters and inner tubes, beach balls,
   Frisbees, and anything else that might be fun at the beach.

5. Prepare the food and keep it in a cooler until time to cook it. You might serve hot dogs, chips, cupcakes or cookies, and sodas. Don't forget the buns and condiments (such as ketchup and mustard).

6. Play games and do activities at the beach, such as:

    Play beach volleyball.

    Play Frisbee or Scoop Toss.

    Have raft races.

    Get into squirt-gun fights.

    Make sand castles.

### Safety Tips

★ Be sure everyone can swim if you go in the water, and have parents watch the swimmers.

★ Don't forget the sunscreen.

★ Try not to get sand in your eyes—or inside your bathing suit!

7. When you're tired and hungry, have your parents light up the hibachi or barbeque and have a cookout.

8. Spread out the beach towels and enjoy your dogs, chips, and sodas.

9. Clean up your section of the beach and head for home.

# Sand Casting

Ages 7 to 12

When you have an endless supply of sand, here's the perfect project that lets you bring some of that sand home in a brand new shape.

## Materials

★ Sand
★ 5-pound bag plaster of Paris
★ Large bucket
★ Stick for stirring
★ Plasticware for shaping sand
★ Cardboard box

## Skills Learned

✔ Reading and following directions
✔ Scientific properties
✔ Cognitive skills/problem solving/cause and effect
✔ Nature studies

## What to Do

1. Find a good spot on the beach.
2. Dampen the sand with water.
3. Think about what you want to design, such as a face, a monster mask, or anything you like.
4. Use your fingers and plasticware to dig into the sand and create a mold. Think about how the design will look after you've poured in the plaster of Paris—it will be in reverse.
5. Form a ridge around the design to keep the plaster in.
6. Mix the plaster according to directions, using the large bucket and stick.
7. Pour the plastic slowly into the sandy mold until it's completely covered.
8. Let the plaster dry, about 15 to 20 minutes.
9. Carefully dig up the design with your fingers, being careful not to damage the design.

**10.** Gently brush away the excess sand and place the mold in the box to keep it safe.

**11.** When it's completely dry, usually the next day, add details to the design with acrylic paint.

---

## More Fun

Add seashells, rocks, or other items to the sand to decorate your sculpture before you pour the plaster. Or make your own fake seashells or sand dollars using small amounts of plaster of Paris covered with sand on both sides.

---

# Sand Painting

Ages 7 to 12

Navajo people developed the art of creating beautiful "paintings" using sand. Add a little color to make your artwork even more fun.

**Materials**
- ★ Light-colored sand
- ★ Several bowls
- ★ Colored sidewalk chalk
- ★ Posterboard
- ★ Pencil
- ★ Newspapers
- ★ Glue and water
- ★ Paintbrush

**Skills Learned**
- ✔ Fine motor development
- ✔ Nature and culture studies
- ✔ Creative and imaginative expression

## What to Do

1. Pour a little sand into each bowl.

2. Color the sand by rubbing a piece of chalk over the grains. (Don't inhale the chalk dust while you work.)

3. Stir the sand to color it evenly.

4. Make several colors of sand.

5. Draw a picture on the posterboard using the pencil. You might draw a nature scene, an Indian design, an animal, or whatever you like.

6. Think about what colors you'd like to use in the different areas of the design. Remember you'll be using sand to "paint" the picture, so make the areas large enough to fill with sand (but not so large that you run out of sand!).

7. Mix a little water with the glue to thin it down.

8. Paint the glue on one area of the design using the paintbrush.

9. Carefully sprinkle one color of sand on the glued area.

10. Allow the area to dry for a few minutes and then carefully turn the picture over onto the newspaper so the excess sand falls onto it.

11. Fold the newspaper in half to collect the sand, and pour the sand back into its bowl.

## More Fun

Use the leftover colored sand to make a Rainbow Sand Jar. Clean out a baby food jar or other small jar and pour a layer of colored sand on the bottom. Repeat with each color until the jar is full to the top. Close the jar securely, and put it on your desk or table as a paperweight or work of art.

**12.** Repeat the process until the picture is complete.

**13.** Allow the sand painting to dry thoroughly, then hang it on your wall.

# Waterscope

Ages 7 to 12

Make your own Waterscope and discover a whole new world under the sea—or lake, or ocean.

## Materials

★ Half-gallon milk carton

★ Scissors

★ Sturdy plastic wrap

★ Electrical tape

## Skills Learned

✔ Scientific properties

✔ Nature study

✔ Following directions

✔ Cognitive skills

## What to Do

**1.** Rinse and dry the milk carton.

**2.** Cut a circle out of the bottom of the milk carton.

**3.** Cover the bottom with a large sheet of plastic wrap, stretching it firmly across the opening and around the sides, to make the lens.

**4.** Tape the plastic wrap securely to the sides of the carton, keeping the wrap stretched taut.

### Safety Tip

Be careful using the scissors and get a parent to help if necessary.

**5.** Open the top spout of the carton to use as the viewer end.

**6.** Place the lens side in the water, being careful not to dip it in too deep.

**7.** Look into the viewer to see what's going on in the water.

# Scoop Toss

Ages 7 to 12

While you're at the beach, play a game of Scoop Toss, also known as Jai Alai.

## Materials

★ Two plastic gallon milk jugs (more if you have more than 2 players)
★ Permanent marker
★ Scissors
★ Electrical tape
★ Tennis ball or rubber ball

## Skills Learned

✔ Gross motor skills and exercise
✔ Eye-hand coordination
✔ Social interaction
✔ Counting and math skills

## How to Play

**1.** Rinse milk jugs thoroughly.

**2.** Using the permanent marker, draw a black line on the side of the jug opposite the handle, shaping it into a curve to make a large scoop. Try to picture it before you draw the line so you visualize the scoop.

**3.** Cut out the scoop following the black line, keeping the edge as smooth as possible.

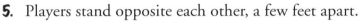

**4.** Cover the cut edge with electrical tape so it isn't sharp.

**5.** Players stand opposite each other, a few feet apart.

**6.** One player places the ball in the scoop and then tosses it to the other player using the scoop.

**7.** The other player must try to catch the ball with his or her scoop.

**8.** Keep throwing the ball using the scoop and count how long you can keep the ball going without missing.

**9.** Stand farther and farther apart as you get better at the game.

## Safety Tips

★ Be careful using the scissors or get a parent to help.

★ Be sure to cover the sharp, rough edges with the tape so they don't cut or scratch anyone.

# 17
# Science Lab

Disco Dancing Bugs

Billions Of Bubbles

Fake Blood

Surf's Up

Volcano Eruption

# Disco Dancing Bugs

Ages 3 to 9

Save a few of these "bugs" to eat while you watch them dance.

## Materials
★ Pint-size clear jar
★ Water
★ 3 to 4 tablespoons vinegar
★ 6 to 8 raisins
★ 1 tablespoon baking soda

## Skills Learned
✔ Scientific properties
✔ Cognitive skills/cause and effect
✔ Following directions

## What to Do
1. Fill the jar with water.
2. Add vinegar and stir.
3. Add the raisins and watch what happens to them.
4. Add the baking soda without stirring and watch what happens.
5. Can you figure out why they "dance"? *(Answer: Bubbles of carbon dioxide form when soda, a base, is mixed with vinegar, an acid. The bubbles cling to the raisins, making them rise and fall for up to an hour.)*
6. Add food coloring for more fun.

### Safety Tip
Be careful to measure the amounts exactly so the jar doesn't overflow!

# Billions of Bubbles

Ages 3 to 12

See how many ways can you make a bubble—or billions of bubbles—from your own bubble factory.

## Materials

★ Bowl or pan
★ Measuring cup
★ Water
★ Liquid detergent
★ Glycerin (available at the pharmacy)
★ Spoon or stick
★ Bubble blowers, such as an empty can, coat hanger, six-pack holder, gardening wire, pipe cleaner, plastic lid, juice can, straws, berry baskets, funnels, and so on

## Skills Learned

✔ Scientific properties
✔ Math and measurement
✔ Cause and effect

## What to Do

1. Using a measuring cup, pour ⅓ cup liquid detergent, ⅓ cup glycerin, and ¼ cup water into a large bowl or pan.
2. Mix well with a spoon or stick.
3. Prepare bubble blowers:

Open a can at both ends, rinse, and make sure there are no sharp edges.

Bend a coat hanger into a circle, square, or diamond shape.

Remove a plastic six-pack holder from soft drinks.

Bend garden wire or pipe cleaners into a variety of creative shapes, making sure the end result creates a closed shape (such as a circle or oval).

Cut the center out of a plastic lid.

Punch a hole in the juice can with a can punch and cut out the bottom.

4. Dip the objects, except the juice can and straw, one at a time into the bubble solution, then wave them in the air to make bubbles.

5. Dip the end of the juice can or straw into the bubble solution, then blow out a bubble using the punched hole at the top.

6. See how many bubble blowers you can make. See how big you can make the bubbles. See how many bubbles you can blow. Try to catch the bubbles using the blowers. Add food coloring to make the bubbles more colorful.

## Safety Tip

Be careful where you put the bubble solution when you're finished, since it can be toxic. Pour it down the sink and rinse the sink well.

# Fake Blood

Ages 7 to 12

Fool and freak out your friends with some fake blood you make in your own kitchen.

## Materials

★ 1½ cups light corn syrup
★ ½ cup grenadine (available at the food store)
★ Bottle of red food coloring
★ 3 drops blue food coloring
★ Glass jar
★ Spoon

## Skills Learned

✔ Creative and imaginative thinking
✔ Understanding scientific properties
✔ Following directions
✔ Cognitive skills/cause and effect
✔ Math and measurement

## What to Do

1. Mix the corn syrup and grenadine.
2. Add a whole bottle of red food coloring (1 fluid ounce) and 3 drops of blue food coloring.
3. Stir well. The mixture should be thick, dark red, and look realistic.
4. Put a few drops of fake blood on your face or hands.
5. Be careful to put the fake blood on

### Safety Tips

★ Don't scare your parents, or you may end up in the emergency ward at the hospital!
★ Don't get the fake blood on good clothes or furniture.

old clothes only, since it soaks in well and could ruin your good clothes.

**6.** Think up ways to use the fake blood and give your friends a thrill.

# Surf's Up

Ages 7 to 12

Watch the calm sea turn into a turbulent ocean when the surf comes up.

## Materials

★ 1 clear, plastic, 32-ounce soda bottle
★ Funnel
★ ½ cup water
★ ½ cup cooking oil
★ ½ cup vinegar
★ Blue food coloring (or other color)
★ Glitter or plastic confetti

## Skills Learned

✔ Understanding scientific properties
✔ Cognitive skills/cause and effect
✔ Following instructions

## What to Do

**1.** Wash the bottle, remove the labels, and dry the bottle.
**2.** Pour water into the bottle using the funnel.
**3.** Pour oil into the bottle using the funnel.
**4.** Pour vinegar into the funnel.
**5.** See what happens as you add the different liquids.

6. Add several drops of blue food coloring and glitter.
7. Close the cap tightly.
8. Shake the bottle to make waves and surf, or swirl it around to create a tornado.

**More Fun**

Buy a "tornado tube" (available at the toy, hobby, nature, or science store) and attach it to the bottle. Clean another bottle and attach it to the other end of the tube. Swirl the water in the bottom bottle, then turn it upside down and watch what happens.

# Volcano Eruption

Ages 7 to 12

Don't blow your top—let the volcano do it with a simple chemical reaction you can concoct in your kitchen.

## Materials
★ Tall, thin jar with lid
★ Baking soda
★ Water
★ Dishwashing liquid
★ Red food coloring
★ Large plastic container, such as a dishpan
★ Dirt
★ Vinegar

## Skills Learned
✔ Scientific experimentation
✔ Cognitive skills/cause and effect
✔ Nature study

## What to Do

1. Pour ¼ cup baking soda, ¼ cup water, and 3 tablespoons dishwashing liquid in the jar.
2. Add a few drops of red food coloring and stir.
3. Cover the jar with the lid.
4. Put the jar in the plastic container.
5. Dampen the dirt and shape it around the jar to form a volcanic mountain. You can also cover the jar with clay, papier-mache, or plaster of Paris and paint it brown to make it look like a real volcano.
6. Remove the lid, quickly pour in ¼ cup vinegar, and watch out as your volcano erupts!

**Safety Tip**

Be careful while pouring in vinegar, which is what causes the reaction.

# 18
# Sports Challenge

Follow the Leader

Water Olympics

Goofy Golf Olympics

Bike Olympics

Flying Frisbees

Stilt Walkers

# Follow the Leader

Ages 3 to 12

It's fun being a leader and watching the other kids following your actions. It's also fun trying to follow the leader.

## Materials
★ Watch or timer

## Skills Learned
✔ Cognitive skills
✔ Creative and imaginative thinking
✔ Social interaction
✔ Gross motor development and exercise

## What to Do
**1.** Choose someone to be the leader.
**2.** The leader must think up creative things to do as he leads the rest of the players, such as hop on one foot, do a somersault, walk backwards, do a silly dance, crawl over or under an obstacle, and so on.
**3.** The rest of the players must imitate everything the leader does.
**4.** When 5 minutes are up, the second person in line becomes the leader and the leader goes to the end of the line.
**5.** Play until everyone has had a turn being the leader.

### Safety Tip
Don't do anything that could endanger the other kids. Keep the stunts safe and fun.

# Water Olympics

Ages 3 to 12

Jump into the pool or lake and have yourself a Water Olympics. Let the games begin.

## Materials
★ Water hose
★ Medium-sized ball

## Skills Learned
✔ Gross and fine motor and exercise
✔ Creative and imaginative thinking
✔ Social interaction
✔ Competence and confidence

## How to Play

### Sprinkler Jump
1. Hold the hose out about a foot from the ground.
2. Turn on the nozzle so the water creates a pole you can jump over.
3. Have players line up and try to jump over the water pole.
4. Keep raising the pole after everyone has had a turn.
5. Play until there's only one player left.

### Water Limbo
1. Hold the hose about 4 feet from the ground.
2. Turn the nozzle on to create a water-limbo pole.
3. Have players line up and try to walk under the pole, leaning backwards, without getting wet.
4. Repeat, lowering the water "pole" each time.
5. Play until there's only one player left.

### Water Waves

1. Hold the hose up in the air about chest high and slowly move the water up and down to create a moving wave.
2. Have players line up and, one at a time, try to run through the water without getting wet.
3. Move the water faster and faster each time the players run through.
4. Play until there's only one player left who didn't get wet.

### Water Snake

1. Hold the hose down on the ground and slowly move it back and forth to create a slithering snake.
2. Players try to run through the water trying not to get their feet wet.
3. Move the water faster and faster each time.
4. Play until there's only one player left who hasn't been "caught" by the water snake.

### Water Jump-Rope

1. Hold the hose up in the air about chest high and turn it like a jump-rope to make large water circles.
2. Players run into the water rope and jump, trying not to get wet.
3. Have players increase their number of jumps each time.
4. Play until there's only one player left who didn't get wet.

### Water Ball

1. Hold the hose up about chest high to serve as a net.
2. Two players stand on either side of the water net and toss a ball back and forth.

## More Fun

Create medals for the winners and award them after each event. (Better make sure they're waterproof, since they're likely to get wet!)

3. While they try to throw and catch the ball, the player holding the water tries to hit the ball with the stream.

4. If the water hits the ball, the person with the hose takes the place of the person who threw the ball and that person is out.

# Goofy Golf Olympics

Ages 7 to 12

You can play Golf Olympics inside or out, as long as you're careful with the balls you use.

## Materials

★ Real or plastic golf clubs or sticks or bats
★ Real golf balls for outside and ping-pong balls for inside area
★ Empty cans
★ Shoeboxes or other small boxes
★ Blocks
★ Books
★ Index cards
★ Markers
★ Sticks
★ Tape

## Skills Learned

✔ Fine and gross motor skills and exercise
✔ Eye-hand coordination
✔ Creative and imaginative thinking
✔ Social interaction

## What to Do

1. Collect some golf clubs or sticks and some golf balls or ping-pong balls.

2. Gather a variety of items to use as "holes," such as the objects listed in Materials and below.

3. Open both ends of the cans and set them on their sides to make open tunnels.

4. Open only one end of the cans and set them on their sides to make closed holes.

5. Cut holes in the boxes to make more tunnels and holes.

6. Set up blocks to make more tunnels and holes.

7. Open an old book or fold some cardboard and set it up like a tent to make a tunnel for the ball to go through.

8. Write numbers on the index cards and tape them to the sticks, then insert them in the ground next to each hole. If you're playing inside, tape the cards to a nearby piece of furniture or wall.

9. Start by hitting the golf ball with the club a few feet away from Hole #1, until you complete the whole course.

10. Keep track of how many strokes it takes you to hit the ball into each hole and add up your total at the end.

## Safety Tip

Don't use a real golf ball in the house, or you might break a window.

# Bike Olympics

Ages 7 to 12

Use your bikes to show off your stunts and win a ribbon at the Bike Olympics.

## Materials

★ Bicycles
★ Sidewalk chalk
★ Wood ramp
★ Brick
★ Cans
★ Bucket
★ Sponges
★ Rolled-up newspaper

## Skills Learned

✔ Physical activity and exercise
✔ Gross motor skills
✔ Cognitive skills
✔ Social interaction

## How to Play

1. Gather your friends and their bikes at an empty parking lot, vacant lot, or safe paved area where you can ride easily. (Don't forget to get permission from your parents.)

2. Set up a number of stunts for the riders to perform, such as:

   Draw a curvy line for the bikes to follow using the sidewalk chalk.

   Build a sloped ramp by laying one end of a wood plank on a brick to use as a jump.

   Set out cans to use as obstacles to slalom around like skiers do.

Set out a bucket and have riders try to toss sponges into the bucket as they ride.

Give one rider a rolled-up newspaper and have her pass it to another rider, then another, until everyone has passed on the newspaper.

**Safety Tips**

★ Make sure the area is a safe place to ride—with no cars nearby or obstacles that may cause an accident or injury.
★ Watch out that you don't crash into one another while you're doing the stunts!

# Flying Frisbees

Ages 7 to 12

Test your skills with a Frisbee and play this challenging game in your backyard or the local park.

## Materials
★ Frisbees
★ Paper plates
★ Markers
★ Nails or duct tape

## Skills Learned
✔ Gross motor skills and exercise
✔ Social interaction and good sportsmanship
✔ Spatial relationships and eye-hand coordination
✔ Cognitive skills

## What to Do

1. Each player must have a Frisbee to play.
2. Number the paper plates from 1 to 9.
3. Look over your playing field for good spots to place your goals.
4. Choose a starting point, then select the first spot for your goal—about 20 to 25 feet away from the starting point.
5. Nail or tape paper plate #1 to a tree, post, or fence, about 4 or 5 feet high.
6. Look around for a good spot to place plate #2, again about 20 to 25 feet away, and hang plate #2.
7. Continue until all 9 plates are in place.
8. Go back to the starting point and throw the Frisbee toward the first goal.
9. If a player hits the plate, he may go on to the next goal.
10. If a player doesn't hit the plate, players take turns picking up their Frisbees where they landed and trying again to hit the goal.
11. Each time a player misses, he loses a point.
12. After 5 tries, take 5 points off and move on to the next goal.
13. Continue playing all 9 goals.
14. Count up the total number of tries to hit the target. The player who has the fewest total tries is the winner.

### More Fun

If a player misses a goal 5 times, have him do a stunt before he moves onto the next goal.

# Stilt Walkers

Ages 7 to 12

Walking on Stilt Walkers is like learning to walk all over again. Once you're up, can you keep from falling down?

## Materials

★ 2 large coffee cans, or similar cans, per person
★ Hammer and nails
★ Scissors
★ 5 yards of rope per person

## Skills Learned

✔ Cognitive skills/problem solving
✔ Math and measurement
✔ Fine and gross motor skills
✔ Social interaction
✔ Competence

## What to Do

1. Get 2 large cans for each player.
2. Turn the cans upside down so the open side is down.
3. Punch a hole on either side of each can, near the bottom, using the hammer and nail.
4. Measure a length of rope from the ground to your waist and double it.
5. Tie each end into either side of one can.

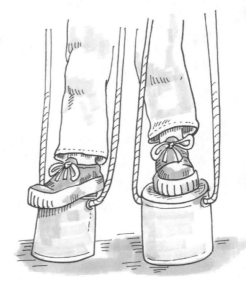

**6.** Repeat for the other can (measure another length of rope and tie it into the other can).

**7.** Put the 2 cans next to each other, about 1 foot apart.

**8.** Carefully step up onto the cans, holding its looped rope with the hand that's on the same side.

**9.** As you take a step with your right foot, pull up on the rope in your right hand, keeping it taut to your foot as you move it forward. Repeat with your left hand and foot, and so on.

**10.** After you practice walking around a while, set up an obstacle course and see if you can race through it.

## More Fun

Put on a pair of Dad's old pants, long enough to cover the ropes and cans, so it looks like you're super tall.

# 19
# Vacation

Take-Along Kit

Restaurant Games

Travel Games

Roadside Collection

Travel Hunt

# Take-Along Kit

Ages 3 to 12

The best way to enjoy your trip is to bring along lots to do so you don't get bored along the way.

## Materials

★ Colored markers
★ Notepad
★ Colored construction paper
★ Scissors
★ Tape
★ Compass
★ Magnifying glass/ binoculars
★ Map
★ Deck of cards
★ Guidebooks
★ Disposable camera
★ Scrapbook/journal
★ Snacks and drinks, such as apples, bananas, peanut butter or cheese and crackers, dried fruit, carrots, cut-up sandwiches, cheese strips, beef jerky, and juice boxes
★ Pillow and blanket
★ Big travel bag or backpack

## Skills Learned

✔ Creative and imaginative thinking
✔ Cognitive skills/problem solving
✔ Resourcefulness and competence
✔ Independence and self-esteem
✔ Math and science skills

## What to Do

1. Gather the materials listed and place them in your travel bag or backpack.

2. As you go, look through your travel bag and pull out a few items to use.

3. Use your imagination and creativity with the materials and think up fun things to do, such as:

   Draw pictures of what you see along your route.

   Take pictures and put them in a scrapbook with captions about your vacation.

   Think up some new card games and tricks.

   Use your binoculars to look at sites up close from the car and your magnifying glass to look at things up close when you're out of the car.

   See how many creative ways you can eat your snacks.

   Make things out of construction paper, such as sunhats, stationery, cootie catchers, paper chains, paper dolls, origami, and so on.

   Use your pillow to take a nap.

### Safety Tip

Be careful when using scissors or other sharp instruments in the car, in case you hit a bump!

# Restaurant Games

Ages 3 to 12

It can be boring waiting for your food in a restaurant while you're on vacation, so try these entertaining games until the meals arrive.

## Materials

★ Restaurant items, such as salt shaker, sugar packet, silverware, butter pats, jelly packs, toothpicks, crackers, napkins, and so on

## Skills Learned

✔ Cognitive skills/problem solving
✔ Social interaction
✔ Language and vocabulary

## What to Do

### Mystery Diner

1. Choose someone in the restaurant to be the Mystery Diner.
2. Give each player one clue to his or her identity, such as a color he's wearing, the way he's sitting, the food he's eating, and so on.
3. See if the other players can guess who it is.
4. Keep giving clues until someone guesses the right answer.

### What's Missing?

1. Set out a number of items on the table, such as the salt shaker, sugar packet, fork, knife, spoon, pat of butter, jelly pack, toothpick, napkin, and so on, and arrange them in a row or circle.

2. Cover the items with a large napkin or have the other players close their eyes.

3. Remove one item from the table, then remove the napkin or have players open their eyes.

4. Players must guess what's missing from the table.

### Pass the Spoon

1. Fill a spoon with sugar.

2. Pass the spoon from player to player, trying not to spill it.

3. Whoever spills any sugar loses the game.

### Jigsaw Cracker

1. Each player breaks a cracker into 5 or 6 small pieces.

2. Pass the pieces to the next player and see who can put their cracker back together first.

3. To make it really hard, mix up all the pieces and see if you can put the crackers back together.

> ### More Fun
>
> Play the Manners Game by using your best manners. Players must watch each other to catch someone using bad manners. If they're caught, they lose a point.

# Travel Games

Ages 3 to 12*

*Note: Alphabet Chat is recommended for ages 7 to 12.*

The best way to make the miles pass is to play travel games with your family, friends, and even by yourself.

## Materials

★ Glass or cup
★ Paper and pencil
★ Spoon
★ Cereal or crackers

## Skills Learned

✔ Reading and writing skills
✔ Cognitive skills
✔ Math and measurement skills
✔ Science exploration
✔ Independence
✔ Social interaction

## What to Do

### Alphabet Chat

1. Choose a topic to discuss with the other players, such as: "What we'll do on our vacation" or "What I miss about leaving home."
2. Choose a random letter of the alphabet to begin the conversation, such as "M."
3. The first player begins the conversation using the selected letter, making sure it's related to the topic. For example, if the topic is "What we'll do on our vacation" and the letter is "M," you might start the conversation like this: "Mom, I can't wait to get there!"
4. The next player must continue the topic with a sentence using the next letter of the alphabet. For example, the next sentence might be, "No one else at my school has been to Disney World before."
5. Continue the topic, moving on to the next letter, and the next, until you're finished with all 26 letters.
6. If anyone gets stuck and can't give a sentence beginning with the next letter, she gets one negative point.
7. Whoever has the fewest misses wins.
8. Choose a new topic and a new letter and play again—until you reach your destination.

## Backseat Stunts

1. Make up a bunch of stunts to perform in the car as you travel to your destination—without taking off your seatbelt—such as:

   Drink a glass of water without spilling.

   Turn around in your seat.

   Find something in the car by description.

   Write something with your toes.

   Identify someone's hand with your eyes closed.

   Put your clothes on backwards.

   Toss a ball and catch it 10 times without letting it go in the front seat area.

   Dance to a song on the radio.

   Press your face to the glass and make another rider laugh.

2. When you've completed your tasks, think up some more.

## Build a House

1. The goal of the game is to be the first to draw a house on paper by finding objects along the route. For example:

   Find a Stop Sign—draw a square.

   Find a bridge—draw a roof.

   Find a police car—draw a front door.

   Find a dog—draw a chimney.

   Find a fast food sign—draw a window.

   Find a baby—draw shutters.

   Find a broken-down car—draw a doorknob.

2. Whoever finishes the house first wins the game.

### Spoon Spill

1. Each player fills a spoon to the top with cereal, crackers, or other small items.
2. Players must hold their spoons steady as they travel and try not to spill the contents when the car goes over bumps and dips.
3. The player who keeps his spoon full the longest wins the game.

### Predictions

1. Each player writes down a number of predictions for the driver, such as:

   | | |
   |---|---|
   | Scratch his head | Forget his blinker is on |
   | Look out the side window | Reach for something |
   | Tell the kids to be quiet | Eat a snack |
   | Adjust the mirror | Exercise his neck |
   | Look at the map | Turn the radio dial |

2. Whenever the driver completes one of the predictions on the list, that player gets to check it off.
3. The player with the most correct predictions is the winner.

### People Watching

1. When you're in an area where there are lots of people, try to find as many of the following items on the people as you can:

   | | |
   |---|---|
   | Woman with a hat | Hawaiian shirt |
   | Person wearing a camera | Sunglasses |
   | Bare feet | Black sweater |
   | Baggy shorts | Logo T-shirt |
   | Long skirt | Bare chest |

2. Whoever finds the most wins the game.

**Bad Driver**

1. Your job is to find as many moving violations as you can within a period of time. For example, can you spot a driver doing any of the following:

Eating while driving

Not using a turn signal

One hand on the steer-
ing wheel

Driving too close

Driving too fast

Forgot to turn off turn
signal

Driving too slow

Changing lanes too many times

Driving without a seatbelt

Driving with a broken tail-light

Talking on the phone while driving

2. At the end of half an hour or so, see who's found the most violations.

> **More Fun**
>
> Think up games you can play using license plates, road signs, landmarks, and other car-related activities.

# Roadside Collection

Ages 7 to 12

Bring your vacation home with you—just remember where you got each sample.

## Materials

★ Large, clear plastic jar with a lid
★ Trowel or large spoon
★ Wax paper
★ Scissors
★ A few old socks
★ Permanent marker
★ Book on the area where you'll be traveling
★ Pad of paper and pencil

## Skills Learned

✔ Geography and geology
✔ Cognitive skills/classification skills
✔ Writing and reporting
✔ Reading and research

## What to Do

1. Prepare for your Roadside Collection before you go on vacation by collecting the materials listed above.
2. Cut out a bunch of circles from waxed paper, using the jar lid as a guide.
3. Begin your collection at home by digging up some dirt from your yard.
4. Spread about an inch of the dirt on the bottom of the jar and smooth it flat.
5. Write on the jar the date and where you got the dirt using the permanent marker.
6. Place a waxed-paper circle on top of the layer to keep it intact.
7. Stuff some old socks on top to keep the dirt in place as you travel.
8. Set the jar in a secure and stable place in the car.
9. Each time you stop somewhere on your trip, for gas, food, or any reason, carefully remove the socks from your

Roadside Collection jar and then dig up more dirt and layer it in the jar, topping it with waxed paper and a sock or two to keep it in place.

**10.** Write the date and place each time you add a layer.

**11.** While you're in each place, see if the guidebook mentions the soil, geography, or geology of the area.

**12.** Write that information on your pad of paper, along with other related information, such as the plants that are growing nearby, the weather, the shape of the terrain or ground, and other things you see.

**13.** When you get home, look at the various layers of dirt and see how similar or different they are.

**14.** Share your Roadside Collection with friends and tell them about each place you visited.

**15.** Make up a story about why each layer is different.

**16.** Collect other things along your vacation route—such as leaves, rocks, flowers, even postcards, restaurant napkins, menus, and other items—to remind you of your trip. Put them in a scrapbook, along with some of your written memories of the trip.

**Safety Tip**

Be careful you dig in a safe place, and don't accidentally dig up some poison oak or uncover some snakes!

# Travel Hunt

Ages 7 to 12

Play a real version of a treasure hunt on your travels and make the trip come alive.

## Materials

★ Map of your vacation
★ Guidebook of your vacation
★ Posterboard
★ Paper and pencil
★ Colored markers
★ Stickers

## Skills Learned

✔ Map reading and geography
✔ Cognitive skills/problem solving
✔ Spatial awareness
✔ Math and measurement

## What to Do

1. Get a map to your destination and a guidebook that covers the trip.
2. On posterboard, draw a game board loosely based on your trip. Make squares that link together into a curving chain, like the game Candyland.
3. Study your map and guidebook and find landmarks, signposts, and attractions along the route, such as towns, rivers, mountains, bridges, amusement parks, tall buildings, names of towns, and so on.
4. On your game board, fill in the squares with the names of the sites in the order you'll find them on your trip.
5. Use the colored markers to make the game board fun and festive. Add illustrations to decorate it further.

6.  Get out your game board and stickers as you begin your trip and start looking for the first landmark.

7.  When you find a landmark, cover it with a sticker.

8.  See how many landmarks you can find along the way.

## More Fun

Make Roadtrip Bingo cards by cutting out squares from posterboard. Draw a 5-square by 5-square grid, then fill in the squares by drawing—or cutting out and pasting on pictures of—items you're likely to find along the route, such as a tree, bird, fire engine, river, bridge, man with hat, fast food restaurant, mall, big boulder, grocery store, and so on. Play with your family or a friend and see who can find five in a row first. Then exchange cards and play again.

# 20
# Water Works

Slippery Slide

Sponge Attack

Water Snake

Bucket Brigade

Kiddy Pool Carnival

Octopus Catch

Pop the Piranha

Swimming Pool Games

# Slippery Slide

Ages 3 to 12

Take a ride on a slippery slide to keep cool on a hot sunny day.

## Materials

★ Several large heavy-duty plastic garbage bags
★ Scissors
★ Electrical tape
★ Tent pegs or large flat stones wrapped in old towels
★ Water, hose, and nozzle

## Skills Learned

✔ Following instructions
✔ Gross motor skills and exercise
✔ Social interaction
✔ Cooperation and taking turns
✔ Creative and imaginative thinking

## How to Play

1. Cut the garbage bags along the sides, lengthwise, so the plastic opens up into a long length for the slide.
2. Tape the ends of the garbage bags together with electrical tape to make an even longer slide.
3. Lay the plastic slide on the lawn and secure the corners using the tent pegs or stones wrapped in old towels.
4. Place the hose with the

nozzle attached at one end of the slide. (If the slide goes downhill, put the hose so the water runs down the hillside.)

5. Turn on the water, adjust the nozzle to the "spray" setting, and make sure the water is running down the slide.

6. Line up and take turns running, slipping, and sliding on the Slippery Slide.

7. Play Follow the Leader and take turns copying each other as you lead the others down the slide. Use your imagination and create some new stunts to perform on the slide.

## Safety Tips

★ Make sure the tent pegs are secure and that no sharp ends are sticking out to hurt someone.

★ If you're using rocks, make sure they stay covered with the towels so if you slide into one you won't get hurt.

★ Allow only one person to slide at a time so you don't crash into each other.

★ Move the slide after an hour of play so your lawn isn't damaged.

# Sponge Attack

Ages 3 to 12

Sponges aren't just for cleaning. Get them wet and give your friends a wet and wild "bath."

## Materials

★ Lots of sponges in a variety of shapes, sizes, and colors
★ Buckets of water
★ Water hose

## Skills Learned

✔ Gross and fine motor development and exercise
✔ Social interaction
✔ Cognitive skills/strategy
✔ Creative and imaginative thinking

## How to Play

1. Buy a bunch of inexpensive sponges in all different sizes and shapes and colors.
2. Fill some buckets with water from the hose and set them around the yard.
3. Toss the sponges into the buckets, equally divided.
4. On the word "Go!" everyone grabs a sponge from a bucket and tries to hit another player by throwing a wet sponge at them to get him or her "out."
5. You can pick up and reuse a sponge by dipping it in the water as long as you only have one sponge at a time. Keep going back for more sponges until there's only one player left in the game.

## More Fun

Divide into teams and see which team can get everyone on the other team out first. Or have the teams try to steal the other team's bucket of sponges without getting tagged by a flying sponge.

# Water Snake

Ages 3 to 12

Watch your back—and front. No matter what you do, you're going to get sprayed by a water snake.

## Materials

★ Garden hose
★ Short stake or broom handle
★ String

## Skills Learned

✔ Quick thinking
✔ Quick reflexes
✔ Gross motor skills and exercise
✔ Social interaction

## How to Play

1. Put on your bathing suit or clothes that can get wet.
2. Stick your stake or broom handle into the grass.
3. Attach a hose to the water spigot and tie the other end of the hose to the top of the stake, allowing a foot or two of the hose to stick out above the stake.
4. Outline a circle around the stake using a length of rope or another hose, marking the boundaries of the snake pit.
5. Turn on the water enough to cause the end of the hose to whip around wildly.
6. Run around the grass, staying inside the boundaries, as you try not to get "snake spit" on you!

### Safety Tip

Make sure the stake has no sharp points or edges sticking up and that you're playing on a grassy area in case you slip and fall down.

# Bucket Brigade

Ages 3 to 12

Fill the kiddy pool in a creative way and then keep cool while you play in the water works.

## Materials

★ Kiddy pool
★ Bucket or pail
★ Water
★ Stopwatch
★ Variety of containers

## Skills Learned

✔ Cognitive skills/problem solving
✔ Cooperation and social interaction
✔ Math, counting, and measurement skills
✔ Gross motor development and exercise

## How to Play

1. Gather your friends in their bathing suits on a hot day.
2. Set the kiddy pool a few feet from the water spigot.
3. Line up the kids from the spigot to the pool at arm's length.
4. Give the first player nearest the spigot a bucket or pail.
5. Have her fill the pail with water and then pass it to the next player in line, who passes it to the next player, until it reaches the pool.
6. The last player pours the water into the pool and then runs back to the spigot to fill the pail again.
7. Continue until the pool is full—which may take a while if the giggling kids keep spilling the bucket of water.

## More Fun

Give everyone a bucket to really get the game—and the water—moving! Using a stopwatch, have the kids pass the water faster and faster each time the bucket moves down the line. Instead of using buckets, try a variety of containers for passing the water, such as an ice-cube tray, a baking pan, a plastic cup, sponges, cans, and so on.

# Kiddy Pool Carnival

Ages 3 to 12

Have you ever gone to a carnival—in the water? Come on in. The water's fun!

## Materials

★ Kiddy pool
★ Full soda or soup cans
★ Plastic rings
★ Coins
★ Frisbees
★ Small balls
★ Bucket
★ Hula Hoop
★ Balloons
★ Large ball

## Skills Learned

✔ Gross and fine motor development
✔ Social interaction
✔ Cognitive skills/problem solving
✔ Eye-hand coordination
✔ Creative and imaginative thinking

## How to Play

### Can Toss

1. Set a number of soda or soup cans in the kiddy pool with the tops sticking above the water's surface.
2. Stand outside the pool and try to throw the rings over the can tops.
3. Or try to toss coins on top of the cans.

### Target Ball

1. Set some plastic rings or face-down Frisbees in the pool.
2. Stand outside the pool and try to toss small balls into the centers of the rings or Frisbees.

### Bucket Ball

1. Fill a bucket with a little water and set it in the pool so it is weighted but will still float.
2. Try to toss the small balls into the bucket from outside the pool.

### Bounce Ball

1. Set the pool by a wall.
2. Stand a few feet from the pool and try to get the balls into the pool by bouncing them off the wall.
3. Make it more difficult by bouncing the balls into a floating Hula Hoop in the pool.

### More Fun

Use your creativity and imagination and think up some other ways to use the kiddy pool for carnival fun.

### Balloon Tag

1. Float a bunch of balloons in the water.
2. Stand outside the pool and try to knock a balloon out of the water by throwing a large ball at it.

# Octopus Catch

### Ages 7 to 12

Can the Octopus catch the ball and save himself from the ocean floor?

## Materials

★ Kiddy pool

★ Water

★ Medium or large beach ball or rubber ball

## Skills Learned

✔ Gross motor skills and exercise

✔ Cognitive skills/quick thinking

✔ Coordination and balance

✔ Social interaction

## How to Play

1. Have the kids sit in a circle around the inside edge of the pool.
2. Tell the Octopus to sit in the middle of the pool.
3. Give the ball to a player sitting in the circle and have her toss it to another player, over the head of the Octopus.
4. The Octopus must try to catch the ball as it flies overhead.
5. Keep tossing the ball to different players until the Octopus finally catches it.
6. Whoever throws the ball that is caught by the Octopus then becomes the Octopus.

## More Fun

Give everyone except the Octopus a small ball and then have everyone throw the balls at the same time while the Octopus tries to catch one of the balls. Watch everyone scramble as they try to catch a ball. The player without a ball is the new Octopus.

# Pop the Piranha

Ages 7 to 12

This game will keep the kids hopping—and popping—and thoroughly soaked.

## Materials

★ Kiddy pool
★ Balloons
★ Permanent black markers

## Skills Learned

✔ Gross motor skills and exercise
✔ Quick thinking
✔ Social interaction
✔ Cognitive skills/problem solving
✔ Creative and imaginative thinking

## How to Play

1. Fill the kiddy pool with water.
2. Blow up a bunch of balloons, at least enough for each player, more if you have them.
3. Have the kids draw piranha faces on the balloons with the markers, being careful not to get the ink on their hands. Encourage them to be creative and make the fish faces scary, with lots of sharp teeth.
4. Put the balloons in the pool.
5. On the word "Go!" have everyone jump into the

### More Fun

Fill balloons with water and have the kids stand opposite each other in pairs. Have them toss the water balloons back and forth to each other, taking a step backwards each time they finish a toss.

pool, get a balloon, and try to pop it by sitting on it. It shouldn't be easy, since the water makes everything slippery.

# Swimming Pool Games

Ages 7 to 12

Head for the swimmin' hole—whether the backyard pool or nearby lake—and play some pool games.

## Materials

### Gold Nugget Dive

★ 10 smooth stones
★ Gold spray paint
★ Permanent black marker

### Butterfinger Ball

★ Large plastic ball
★ Sun-protection lotion

### High and Dry

★ Stones or cotton balls or marshmallows or piece of cloth—things that change when they get wet.

## Skills Learned

✔ Gross motor development
✔ Social skills
✔ Cognitive skills
✔ Following directions

## How to Play

### Gold Nugget Dive

1. Find 10 smooth stones about the size of walnuts.
2. Spray paint the stones with gold paint and allow them to dry.

3. Turn your back to the water and throw the gold nuggets in.

4. On the word "Go!" players jump or dive into the pool and try to retrieve as many stones as possible.

5. The player who retrieves the most nuggets win.

6. Throw the nuggets back in and play again.

## Butterfinger Ball

1. Put a little sun-protection lotion on your hands.

2. One player stands on a diving board (or edge of the pool) while the other players stand on the side of the pool (or other side of the pool).

3. As the player jumps off the board, another player on the side of the pool throws the ball to the jumper, who tries to catch it before he hits the water.

4. Take turns throwing and catching the Butterfinger Ball.

## High and Dry

1. Give each player an object that changes when it gets wet, such as one of the items listed in Materials.

2. Have players line up at one end of the pool or lake, holding their objects out of the water.

3. On the word "Go!" players must swim or hop to the other side without getting their objects wet.

4. The first one to reach the finish line with a still-dry object wins the game.

### Safety Tip

Make sure all players can swim or that they stay in shallow water, and have parents supervise the water play.

# Resources

## Codes and Languages

**Braille**

|  | a | b | c | d | e | f | g | h | i | j |
|---|---|---|---|---|---|---|---|---|---|---|
| # | 1 | 2 | 3 | 4 | 5 | 6 | 7 | 8 | 9 | 0 |

| k | l | m | n | o | p | q | r | s | t |
|---|---|---|---|---|---|---|---|---|---|

| u | v | w | x | y | z |
|---|---|---|---|---|---|

## Morse Code

| | | |
|---|---|---|
| A ·— | J ·——— | S ··· |
| B —··· | K —·— | T — |
| C —·—· | L ·—·· | U ··— |
| D —·· | M —— | V ···— |
| E · | N —· | W ·—— |
| F ··—· | O ——— | X —··— |
| G ——· | P ·——· | Y —·—— |
| H ···· | Q ——·— | Z ——·· |
| I ·· | R ·—· | |

## American Sign Language

# Reading Adventures

Here are some of the best books to read during the summer.

*Absolutely Normal Chaos* by Sharon Creech

*Amber Brown Is Not a Crayon* by Paula Danziger

*Anne of Green Gables* by L. M. Montgomery

*Babe: The Gallant Pig* by Dick King-Smith

*Because of Winn-Dixie* by Kate DiCamillo

*Bloomability* by Sharon Creech

*Blubber* by Judy Blume

*The Borrowers* by Mary Norton

*Bud, Not Buddy* by Christopher Paul Curtis

*Bunnicula* by Deborah Howe

*The Castle in the Attic* by Elizabeth Winthrop

*Charlie and the Chocolate Factory* by Roald Dahl

*Chocolate Fever* by Robert Kimmel Smith

*Danny the Champion of the World* by Roald Dahl

*Dear Mr. Henshaw* by Beverly Cleary

*Frindle* by Andrew Clements

*Fudge-a-Mania* by Judy Blume

*The Giver* by Lois Lowry

*Harriet the Spy* by Louise Fitzhugh

*Harry Potter and the Sorcerer's Stone* by J. K. Rowling

*Harvey Angell* by Diana Hendry

*Haunted Summer* by Betty Ren Wright

*Holes* by Louis Sachar

*The Houdini Box* by Brian Selznick

*How to Eat Fried Worms* by Thomas Rockwell

*The Indian in the Cupboard* by Lynne Reid Banks

*Island of the Blue Dolphins* by Scott O'Dell

*James and the Giant Peach* by Roald Dahl

*Judy Moody* by Megan McDonald

*The Jungle Book* by Rudyard Kipling

*The Lion, the Witch and the Wardrobe* by C. S. Lewis

*Little House in the Big Woods* by Laura Ingalls Wilder

*Martin's Mice* by Dick King-Smith

*My Father's Dragon* by Ruth Stiles Gannett

*Number the Stars* by Lois Lowry

*The Original Adventures of Hank the Cowdog* by
    John R. Erickson

*The Phantom Tollbooth* by Norman Juster

*Pippi Longstocking* by Astrid Lindgren

*Poppy* by Brian Floca Avi

*Redwall* by Brian Jacques

*Sammy Keyes and the Hotel Thief* by Wendelin Van Draanen

*School's Out* by Johanna Hurwitz

*The Secret Garden* by Frances Burnett

*Stone Fox* by John Reynolds Gardiner

*The Summer I Shrank My Grandmother* by Elvira Woodruff

*Tales of a Fourth Grade Nothing* by Judy Blume

*Tuck Everlasting* by Natalie Babbitt

*When Zachary Beaver Came to Town* by Kimberly Willis Holt

*The Witches* by Roald Dahl

*The Wonderful Wizard of Oz* by L. Frank Baum

*A Wrinkle in Time* by Madeleine L'Engle

*A Year Down Under* by Richard Peck

# Boredom Buster Quickies

- Learn to whistle
- Study the clouds
- Make lemonade from scratch
- Sit under a tree
- Read a book
- Make a picture album
- Draw yourself
- Take a bubble bath
- Go for ice cream
- Collect recyclables
- Learn sign language
- Have a tea party
- Make a drum from an oatmeal container
- Play glasses filled with water
- Study ants
- Study the stars
- Make a terrarium
- Go on a bike trek
- Write to a pen pal
- Decorate your things with glitter
- Set up an aquarium
- Memorize some jokes and riddles
- Have a talent show
- Go to a museum
- Ask parents for childhood memories
- Exercise to music
- Take a hike
- Write for free stuff
- Keep a journal
- Learn something new
- Wrap your coins
- Put up glow-in-the-dark stars
- Have a picnic
- Have a party
- Put on a magic show
- Be a spy for a day
- Have a squirt-gun war
- Paint your own ceramics
- Put on a mystery play

# Index